The Complete Year in Reading and Writing

Daily Lessons • Monthly Units • Yearlong Calendar

Jaime Margolies and Pam Allyn

SCHOLASTIC

NEW YORK • TORONTO • LONDON • AUCKLAND • SYDNEY
MEXICO CITY • NEW DELHI • HONG KONG • BUENOS AIRES

To all first-grade teachers, who care so much, and:

To my parents, who have taught me the importance
of always putting forth your best effort, working hard,
loving what you do, and how learning is a lifelong journey.
~ *Jaime Margolies*

To Lois Bridges and Danny Miller
~ *Pam Allyn*

Scholastic Inc. grants teachers permission to photocopy the activity and stationery pages from this book for classroom use only. No other part of this publication may be reproduced in whole or in part, or stored in a retrieval system, or transmitted in any form or by any means, electronic, mechanical, photocopying, recording, or otherwise, without written permission of the publisher. For information regarding permission, write to Scholastic Inc., 557 Broadway, New York, NY 10012.

Cover design by Jay Namerow

Interior design by Maria Lilja

Photos by LitLife Archives (interior and cover), Maria Lilja (inside cover)

Acquiring Editor: Lois Bridges

Development and Production Editor: Danny Miller

Copy Editor: Carol Ghiglieri

ISBN 13: 978-0-545-04634-3

ISBN 10: 0-545-04634-3

Copyright © 2008 by LitLife Publishing LLC

Contents

As a bonus, use our Spotlight Units to journey through day-by-day lessons in all the Complete 4 components.

Acknowledgments

We would like to thank the teachers, the children, and our colleagues in the LitLife network of schools who believe in the power of words.

There was a team of people who gave of themselves in the deepest and most generous of ways throughout this project. We are full of gratitude for the wise and thoughtful Delia Coppola, Janet Knight, Debbie Lera, and Michelle Yang. Their insights, feedback, and creations glow brightly throughout this series.

We are grateful for the support of our extraordinary LitLife team: the remarkable and talented Jenny Koons who understands life and people and kids and curriculum and who enriched the books with her careful eye, and the marvelous Rebekah Coleman, whose spirit kept us going and whose wise attention completed us. With thanks to our dedicated interns Jen Estrada and Alyssa McClorey, and to Deb Jurkowitz, LitLife grammarian and in-house linguist. We deeply appreciate our agent, the magical Lisa DiMona, for shining the light that guides our way.

Danny Miller may very well be one of the funniest people on earth. He is also a brilliant editor. His dedicated efforts to this series are appreciated beyond compare by us all. Lois Bridges: inspiration, mentor, friend, champion of children and humanistic education, connector of all dots, editor extraordinaire, we thank you. All our appreciation to the team at Scholastic: the creative Maria Lilja, and Terry Cooper for her vision and dedication to the work of supporting teachers. In addition, we thank Eileen Hillebrand for her genius way of getting the word out there and Susan Kolwicz for her genius in getting the message heard.

This experience of writing six books together has been by turns precious, wild, funny, exhausting, scary, joyous, and deeply satisfying. We collectively gave birth to three babies during this process, visited hundreds of schools, took our own kids to school, and tried to have dinner with our husbands once in a while. From the beginning, we committed to one another that when the work felt hard we would always remember that relationships come first. We are most proud of this and hope our readers can feel the power of our bonds in every page of every book in this series. We thank one another, always.

Pam Allyn sends her boundless gratitude to Jim, Katie, and Charlotte Allyn for their love and for their countless inspirations. She would also like to thank her coauthor Jaime Margolies for her extraordinary commitment to children and her zest and spirit for life.

Jaime Margolies would like to thank the following teachers at Concord Road Elementary School: Mary Jane Amato, Emily Baker, Stacey Buerkle, Leslie Cohen, Alexis Golklang, Rosemarie Marcus, Marilyn Orfinger, Karen Sargis, Heather Schlosser, and Susan Zucchero and the teachers she has worked with at Ridge Street Elementary School, for piloting many of the units in this book and their encouragement and support throughout the process. A special thanks to Erin Rivelli, an amazing friend and colleague. Her creative vision, cheering nature, and thoughtfulness helped to make each of these units even more comprehensive and successful. Jaime would also like to thank the administrators who have supported her and encouraged her to be a lifelong learner especially Shelley Cohen, Margaret Ruller, Lauren Allan, and Layne Hudes. She would like to thank her coauthor Pam Allyn for working with her on this amazing journey. Her vision for teachers and children everywhere is an inspiration to all. She would also like to thank her parents Marilyn and Bob and her brother Jeffrey for their constant encouragement. And last but most important, she would like to thank her loving, supportive husband Aaron and new daughter Ellie, the loves of her life. They made the writing of this book possible.

Chapter 1

All About the Complete Year

Dear First-Grade Teacher,

In much of the best children's literature, many of the young characters seem to be around or in first grade. Think of the Frances books by Russell Hoban, Else Minarik's Little Bear books, or *Sheila Rae, the Brave* and *Chrysanthemum* by Kevin Henkes. For those of you who love teaching first grade, this does not surprise you. The time children spend in that first-grade year is transcendent. Your students are in a constant state of awakening, the dawn of consciousness. Most of what happens this year will form their first conscious memories of school, memories they will keep for the rest of their lives. How wise of these fine writers to place their characters in that context: wide-awake, lively minds, deep in the process of creating memory banks and building a sense of themselves.

First graders are hovering between home and school. They have one foot still in early childhood, one foot in later childhood. Thumbs creep near their mouths during the school day, and even pop in on occasion. And yet they wear a pair of new sneakers to school, practicing their balance on the wall of the playground. They are becoming big kids.

Like Frances and Little Bear, first graders long for the warmth of a mother's or father's or grandmother's arms. Like Frances and Little Bear, they unpack their own lunch at school and put everything away; they can zip up their jackets and spend hours making pretend worlds outside.

The process work we do this year is about helping them build independence as they emerge as readers and writers. The biggest thing of all that we hope and will strive toward in this seminal year is that our children will all learn to read. What a year. What a time. Never to be forgotten—the basis for all that comes after. So the work we do together is about savoring this time—what environments are just right for reading and writing, and how to make choices from all those books and all the potential topics.

First graders love to dig into dress-up boxes and try on personas—first a princess, then a witch. We will study a variety of genres this year, trying on all these ways of being in the world—first storymakers, then sharers of information, then weavers of poetic language.

First graders build forts from blocks and make things out of paper and boxes and use all the found objects in their worlds to make other worlds. They are strategic and thoughtful. In this year we weave in many opportunities for them to develop their strategic skills as readers and writers, helping them to make plans, write books, and make connections across texts.

Finally, first graders are wild for conventions. They cannot get over the magic of the ellipses, the wonder of a comma. They are trying out new techniques because they *can*. This year will include plentiful opportunities to study these conventions, which bring children's own writing to life and help students read with fluency.

Recently we were talking to a first grader. He was telling us all about his day at school and as he did so, he was snapping his front finger and his thumb together: snap, snap, snap. We asked, "Did you just learn how to do that?" He nodded and grinned, so pleased we noticed (even though he was snapping madly right in front of our faces!). This is the essence of the first grader: telling stories while practicing skills.

Join us on this journey into the world of first-grade literacy: the combination of magic and reality and newfound skills and powers, with the sheen of babyhood still upon them.

Warmly,

Jaime Margolies   Pam Allyn

At-a-Glance Overview of the Complete Year

Organized around the Complete 4 components (Process, Genre, Strategy, and Conventions) and four unit stages (Immersion, Identification, Guided Practice, and Commitment), each book in the Complete Year series features a year's worth of integrated reading and writing curriculum. Because we honor your professional decision-making, you will find that the Complete Year provides a flexible framework, easily adapted to your state standards and to the needs and goals of your community, your students, and your teaching style.

What Will You Find Inside the Complete Year Series?

Yearlong Curricular Calendar

Units of Study

- Over 25 detailed unit outlines spanning every season of the school year
- 8 Spotlight Units including more than 100 day-by-day lessons
- 2 ARCH units to start your year right
- 2 reflective units to end your year on a powerful note

Assessment

- Individualized assessments for every unit
- Complete 4 Assessment (C4A)

Lists of Anchor Texts for Each Unit

Parent Letters

Resource Sheets and Homework Assignments

Professional Reading Lists

Glossary of Terms

DVD that features Pam Allyn sharing the benefits of the Complete 4 for the Complete Year as well as ALL downloadable assessment forms and resources. You will also find helpful links to professional development support from LitLife and easy-to-use technological support from RealeBooks to help you publish your students' work.

Pam Allyn's *The Complete 4 for Literacy* and Debbie Lera's *Writing Above Standard* are foundational texts for the Complete Year. LitLife and RealeBooks provide innovative professional and technological support for the Complete Year.

The Complete Year Supports...

Individual teachers wanting a clear road map and detailed lessons for reading and writing and for reading/writing connections.

School or district teams wanting to plan a continuum together with specific lessons and units that address the needs of all students—ELL, gifted, and special needs.

Administrative leaders and literacy coaches wanting to guide their school to a consistent, standards-rich plan for reading and writing instruction.

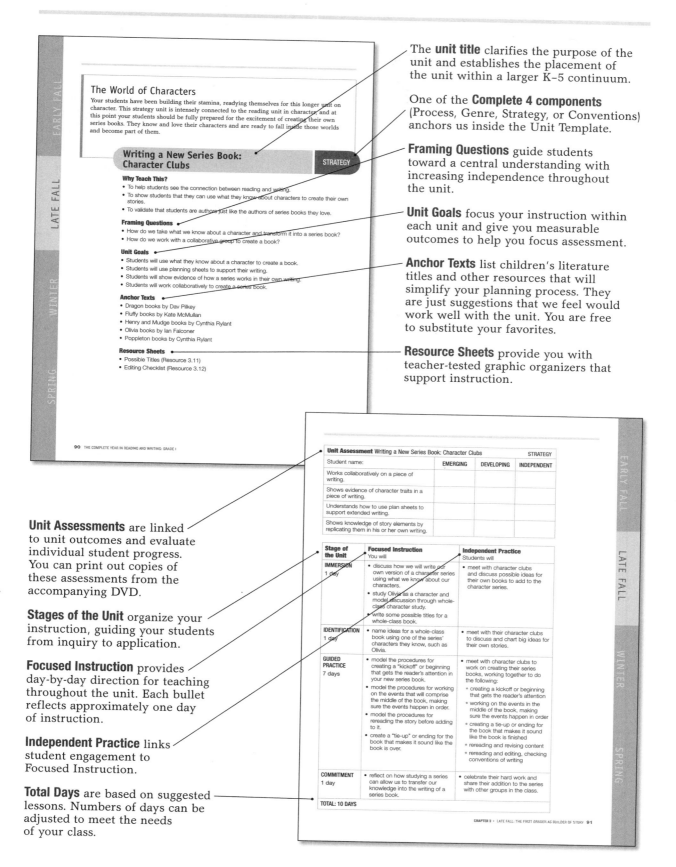

The **unit title** clarifies the purpose of the unit and establishes the placement of the unit within a larger K–5 continuum.

One of the **Complete 4 components** (Process, Genre, Strategy, or Conventions) anchors us inside the Unit Template.

Framing Questions guide students toward a central understanding with increasing independence throughout the unit.

Unit Goals focus your instruction within each unit and give you measurable outcomes to help you focus assessment.

Anchor Texts list children's literature titles and other resources that will simplify your planning process. They are just suggestions that we feel would work well with the unit. You are free to substitute your favorites.

Resource Sheets provide you with teacher-tested graphic organizers that support instruction.

Unit Assessments are linked to unit outcomes and evaluate individual student progress. You can print out copies of these assessments from the accompanying DVD.

Stages of the Unit organize your instruction, guiding your students from inquiry to application.

Focused Instruction provides day-by-day direction for teaching throughout the unit. Each bullet reflects approximately one day of instruction.

Independent Practice links student engagement to Focused Instruction.

Total Days are based on suggested lessons. Numbers of days can be adjusted to meet the needs of your class.

The World of Characters

Your students have been building their stamina, readying themselves for this longer unit on character. This strategy unit is intensely connected to the reading unit in character, and at this point your students should be fully prepared for the excitement of creating their own series books. They know and love their characters and are ready to fall inside those worlds and become part of them.

Writing a New Series Book: Character Clubs — STRATEGY

Why Teach This?
- To help students see the connection between reading and writing.
- To show students that they can use what they know about characters to create their own stories.
- To validate that students are authors just like the authors of series books they love.

Framing Questions
- How do we take what we know about a character and transform it into a series book?
- How do we work with a collaborative group to create a book?

Unit Goals
- Students will use what they know about a character to create a book.
- Students will use planning sheets to support their writing.
- Students will show evidence of how a series works in their own writing.
- Students will work collaboratively to create a series book.

Anchor Texts
- Dragon books by Dav Pilkey
- Fluffy books by Kate McMullan
- Henry and Mudge books by Cynthia Rylant
- Olivia books by Ian Falconer
- Poppleton books by Cynthia Rylant

Resource Sheets
- Possible Titles (Resource 3.11)
- Editing Checklist (Resource 3.12)

90 THE COMPLETE YEAR IN READING AND WRITING: GRADE 1

Unit Assessment Writing a New Series Book: Character Clubs — STRATEGY

Student name:	EMERGING	DEVELOPING	INDEPENDENT
Works collaboratively on a piece of writing.			
Shows evidence of character traits in a piece of writing.			
Understands how to use plan sheets to support extended writing.			
Shows knowledge of story elements by replicating them in his or her own writing.			

Stage of the Unit	Focused Instruction You will	Independent Practice Students will
IMMERSION 1 day	• discuss how we will write our own version of a character series using what we know about our characters. • study Olivia as a character and model discussion through whole-class character study. • write some possible titles for a whole-class book.	• meet with character clubs and discuss possible ideas for their own books to add to the character series.
IDENTIFICATION 1 day	• name ideas for a whole-class book using one of the series' characters they know, such as Olivia.	• meet with their character clubs to discuss and chart big ideas for their own stories.

GUIDED PRACTICE
7 days
	• model the procedures for creating a "kickoff" or beginning that gets the reader's attention in your new series book.
	• model the procedures for working on the events that will comprise the middle of the book, making sure the events happen in order.
	• model the procedures for rereading the story before adding to it.
	• create a "tie-up" or ending for the book that makes it sound like the book is over.
		• meet with character clubs to work on creating their series books, working together to do the following:
		  ° creating a kickoff or beginning that gets the reader's attention
		  ° working on the events in the middle of the book, making sure the events happen in order
		  ° creating a tie-up or ending for the book that makes it sound like the book is finished
		  ° rereading and revising content
		  ° rereading and editing, checking conventions of writing

COMMITMENT 1 day	• reflect on how studying a series can allow us to transfer our knowledge into the writing of a series book.	• celebrate their hard work and share their addition to the series with other groups in the class.
TOTAL: 10 DAYS		

CHAPTER 3 • LATE FALL: THE FIRST GRADER AS BUILDER OF STORY 91

How This Book Will Support You

The Complete Year in Reading and Writing: Grade 1 is written by two authors: Jaime Margolies, a team leader at LitLife and experienced classroom teacher, and Pam Allyn, the executive director of LitLife. Together, we have spent thousands of hours in first-grade classrooms, pondering the unique experience that comprises this year.

LitLife is a global organization dedicated to teacher training in the area of literacy education. Every lesson in this book has been field tested in a wide variety of classrooms. LitLife team leaders coach teachers and work alongside students to create a practical, meaningful curriculum that is well suited to each grade level because it exists inside a broader continuum. See this book as a compass you can use to chart a course in reading and writing instruction that feels true to your beliefs about the developmental needs and interests of first graders.

Many programs do not differentiate sufficiently by grade level. First-grade teachers are often combined into a K–2 grouping in professional literature and workshops. And yet the span between these grades is gigantic psychologically, socially, and intellectually. A curriculum for first grade needs to match the development of the learner and the uniqueness of this age student.

In creating this book for you, we also keep in mind the entirety of the child's learning experience throughout the elementary grades. While specifically written for first graders, the units presented here were created with the big picture in mind, children's entire K–5 experience.

The Complete 4

The Complete 4 was devised in response to the need expressed to us by teachers for balance in literacy instruction. We believe students should be well-rounded readers and writers. This means they should learn about reading and writing strategies. They should also develop a strong understanding of genre and a working knowledge of the conventions of the English language and begin to take on the passions, habits, and behaviors of lifelong readers and writers. The Complete 4 includes four key components of literacy instruction that will help us teach into these varied expectations: Process, Genre, Strategy, and Conventions.

The Complete 4 components help us to plan the school year by balancing the types of units across the year. Knowing whether a unit falls under the category of Process, Genre, Strategy, or Conventions, helps us to focus the unit, so that all our lessons lead up to several key understandings.

Here is what we mean by the Complete 4:

Process	Your students will practice the processes shared by all successful readers and writers, at an appropriate developmental level. These include fluency, stamina, and independence.
Genre	Your students will learn to identify and use various literary containers, including narrative, nonfiction, poetry, and standardized tests.
Strategy	Your students will learn to be strategic as readers and writers, practicing how writers make plans on a page, and how readers approach text differently depending on their needs.
Conventions	Your students will learn grammar and punctuation in contexts that are real, practical, and relevant to their reading and writing experiences.

In planning a Complete Year of literacy instruction for first grade, we have created reading and writing units that reflect a deep balance. All four Complete 4 components are represented. Take a look at the color-coded calendar on the inside front cover of this book to see how these units are organized across the year. We have arranged them so that they build on one another.

Will this book help me connect other aspects of the curriculum to the Complete 4?

Absolutely! One of the best features of the Complete 4 system is its flexibility. It has the capacity to help you integrate all these areas of your curriculum. If you are studying marine animals with your students in April, then you may want to pair your unit with ours in nonfiction reading and writing. If you like to read fairytales with your children, pair that exploration with our units on reading or writing fiction. If you like to study themes, you can pair them with our partnership units so students can meet and talk more deeply about the topics you are studying. You can teach the skills and strategies for reading and writing in the content areas inside one or more of these units. This book will help you forge these connections, and our sample units will give you the resources to make those connections successfully and comfortably.

Alignment to standards is critical, and these units are constructed in such a way as to reflect the standards and to allow for your adjustments for your state standards.

Can this book help me if I have other demands in my day and cannot teach all the units?

Yes, it can. Here are three suggestions for how you could adapt this calendar to your particular situation:
- You can choose one reading and one writing unit from each Complete 4 component to teach during the year.
- You can focus on the units of study that pair well with your existing themes.
- You can teach only the reading or writing strand.

Will the Complete 4 help me forge reading and writing connections with my students?

This is another great aspect of the Complete 4 program: we link reading and writing units as "companions." Although the instruction may not always be identical, the units should be "talking" to one another. You will see how we take special care to make sure reading and writing units echo and parallel each other, or to stagger them so students see, feel, and understand those essential connections. Indeed, reading and writing are interrelated processes that are mutually supportive when taught together. You may have noticed that your strongest writers are typically your most passionate readers.

Can I use this book to support just my writing instruction since I already use another reading program?

Yes. You can use this book to guide you in either reading or writing. Take a look at the writing calendar only; with your grade-level team, you can look into your reading program and see where you can link the writing units into your instruction. For example, if your reading program has a set of stories on friendship, you could link that set to our Writing a New Series: Character Clubs unit in the late fall. This calendar is designed so that you can use it flexibly—you can use either the reading calendar or the writing calendar on its own or if you want the "complete" package, you can use both of them together. And the Complete 4 is also a way to reintroduce quality children's literature into your classroom even if you use a core reading program.

Can I still benefit from this yearlong approach if my school has commitments that must be addressed at different times of the year?

One of the most exciting aspects of the Complete 4 is that the reading and writing units are interconnected and follow a logical sequence. However, we have also constructed the calendars to allow for flexibility. If, for example, your standardized testing comes earlier in the year, you can easily move units around to suit your test preparation schedule. Or if your entire school studies poetry together in the fall rather than the spring, you can move the units to accommodate that. The calendar is designed to be used either as a whole unit, as a step-by-step program, or as building blocks to construct your own unique program.

Will the Complete 4 help me meet the needs of all learners in my classroom?

The range of ability levels and learning modalities in each of our classrooms reminds us to balance our own teaching. The Complete 4 can help us accomplish this. For example, we tend to work with our English language learners mostly on conventions of print, while we work with writers whose first language is English more on strategies or genre. The Complete 4 reminds us that our English language learners flourish with exposure to the habits and passions of readers and writers, the study of different genres, and practice with complex strategies. Similarly, your students who have a comparatively strong sense of conventions are often not given intensive instruction in that area, but they too would enjoy and benefit greatly from inspiring lessons on the construction of a sentence or the artful use of a punctuation mark. The Complete 4 guides us to teach with an eye to creating a Complete Year for all students.

Will this book help me with the flow of my day?

Yes! We are very aware of your time constraints and the benefits of predictable routines. We have created a very simple, easy-to-follow outline for each day's work during reading and writing time that follows a whole/small/whole pattern. These are the three parts of every lesson:

- Focused Instruction: the whole-class lessons
- Independent Practice: individualized or small group work
- Wrap-Up: more whole-class teaching with planning for the next day's lesson

Focused Instruction	Students gather for a period of Focused Instruction for 5 to 15 minutes.
	• Warm up your students with a reference to prior teaching and learning.
	• Teach one clear point.
	• Ask students to quickly try your point.
	• Clarify your teaching point.
	• Set the stage for Independent Practice.
Independent Practice	Students practice independently while you confer with students and/or conduct small instructional groups.
	• Encourage students to read or write independently (at their level).
	• Have students practice your teaching point as they read and write.
	• Meet with individual students, partnerships, and/or groups regularly for informal assessment and instruction.
	• Look for future teaching points or an example to use in the Wrap-Up.
Wrap-Up	Students return for a focused, brief discussion that reflects on the day's learning.
	• Restate your teaching point.
	• Share examples of students' work or learning.
	• Set plans for the next day and make connections to homework.

What are my students actually doing during Independent Practice?

As you will see from the scripted lessons in our Spotlight Units, during Independent Practice, students practice a skill you have demonstrated. In addition, they are doing something that seems fairly simple on the surface but in fact is the heart of our work and the driving energy for all the lessons in this book: **They are reading and writing independently**, every day. We suggest that 50 percent of all reading and writing time is Independent Practice. Of this time, approximately 20 percent should be spent practicing a specific skill associated with their reading, and 80 percent of the time should be spent actually reading and writing! Students should be given time every day to read and write in a comfortable manner, at their reading and writing levels, and in books and topics that are of great personal interest to them. Here are the approximate amounts of time your students can and should be reading and writing for each day (you may have to work toward these minutes as the year unfolds):

Grade Level	Actual Reading Time	Actual Writing Time
KINDERGARTEN	10–15 minutes	10–20 (writing/drawing)
FIRST GRADE	10–20	10–20
SECOND GRADE	20–30	20–25
THIRD GRADE	30–40	25–30
FOURTH GRADE	35–45	25–30
FIFTH GRADE	40–45	30–40

Are there essential materials I must use in order to make the Complete 4 program a success?

You can use any of your support materials, including a core reading program or a phonics program, alongside the Complete 4 approach. The heart of our approach is that every child has time to practice skills, strategies, and processes through reading and writing that is at his level and is as authentic as possible. A seminal National Endowment for the Arts study (2007) found, not surprisingly, that "students who read for fun nearly every day performed better on reading tests than those who reported reading never or hardly at all." The study points to the "failure of schools and colleges to develop a culture of daily reading habits." In addition, an analysis of federal Department of Education statistics found that those students who scored lower on all standardized tests lived in homes with fewer than ten books. (Rich, 2007). This study then points to two pivotal factors in ensuring lifelong literacy: children must have time to read a lot, and children must have easy, continual access to books.

Our work throughout this book and this series is designed to focus on daily Independent Practice: Students are reading authentic literature and reading a lot, every day, at their own level. Students are writing about topics of authentic interest and writing a lot, every day, at their own level. Students are navigating texts and have easy access to understandable texts throughout the day, especially during literacy time. These, then, are the two keys to our work: giving students time to practice reading and writing, and giving them access to texts that inspire them both as readers and as writers.

The access is critical and is best accomplished by establishing a well-stocked classroom library. Your library should have a variety of genres: nonfiction, fiction, and poetry. Approximately 20 to 30 percent of your library should be leveled in a clearly organized system in which children can find books that are truly comfortable for them to read at their independent reading levels.

Your students should have a way to bring their books between home and school and to store the stack of books they have been reading most recently, either in baggies or baskets. Organization is one of two keys to life (the other being passion!).

Don't let disorder get in the way of helping your children do a lot of reading in your classroom. They can help you organize your library, too.

It is also crucial for students to have a way to record thinking about reading, either in a reading notebook, or a folder, or even a binder. The important thing to remember is that this should be a system that works for you and your students. It does not matter so much what you select or what you call it, as long as you know your children can easily access it, they feel comfortable writing in it, and, if they are our youngest readers and writers, drawing in it.

During writing time, your students need order as well. Keep a separate writing area neat and stocked, equipped with all the helpful tools a writer loves: sticky notes, staplers, tape, and date stamps. And as with reading time, your students should have a clearly identified, easy-to-use container to capture their writing. In this series, we use writing notebooks with our students from second grade to fifth grade, and writing folders with students in kindergarten and first grade. Using folders allows us to provide our students with a variety of paper choices if they need them. The key to keeping containers for students' writing work is that it is easy for them to revisit, reread, and reflect upon, and it is easy for you to look at before conferences and to assess on an ongoing basis. Again, it does not matter what you call these containers, or which ones you choose, as long as they are truly useful for both you and your students.

I don't have access to all the anchor texts you recommend in this book or there are other texts I prefer to use instead. Will my units be as effective if my anchor text selections are somewhat different from yours?

We want to give you as many specific suggestions as we can and so we have recommended many anchor texts for each unit. You can find them both in the unit templates and also in the back of the book in a seasonally organized bibliography so you can order all of them for your classroom library if you wish. However, if you can't find them all, or you have others you wish to use instead, you are more than welcome and the units will absolutely be as successful. Take a close look at why we chose the texts we did so you can replace them with selections that will still match the outcomes for the units and will feel comfortable for you.

I use the elements of balanced literacy: shared reading, guided reading, read-aloud, and more. Where do they fit in to the Complete 4 system?

See your elements of balanced literacy as the "how" of your teaching and the Complete 4 as the "what." Teachers who use balanced literacy elements are still asking: But WHAT do I teach tomorrow? The Complete 4 answers that age-old question. Your balanced literacy structures, then, can truly become the engines that drive your content home. For example, shared reading and the read aloud are structures you can use present your content, both in the Focused Instruction and in the Wrap-Up. Guided reading is a structure you can use to practice content with smaller groups of children. This can be done during Independent Practice, so while some of your children are reading independently others are meeting with you in small groups.

What if I've never taught in units like this before?

In a Complete Year unit of study, students learn about one aspect of reading or writing (Process, Genre, Strategy, or Conventions) in a one- to six-week cycle of learning. Inside this book, you will find all the units for a Complete Year of reading and writing instruction. In each unit, we have set a specific focus for instruction and created framing questions to guide you and your students. We have set a time frame and established goals for each unit, and we put together a list of anchor texts that you can use to teach the lessons. Most important, we have provided helpful templates to take you through *all* the units.

To help you implement and pace your instruction, we have divided the instruction in each unit into four key lesson stages: Immersion, Identification, Guided Practice, and Commitment. The premise behind this concept was inspired by the work of Pearson and Gallagher (1983). They delineated a gradual release of responsibility from teacher to student as the ideal conditions for learning. These stages help us make the necessary turns in our teaching so that we move in an efficient and effective way through any unit of study and our students have the best chance for success.

Immersion	We immerse our students in a topic of study.
Identification	We name or define what students must know about the topic by the end of the unit.
Guided Practice	We model reading and writing for our students and give them time for practice, so that we can guide them toward the goals of the unit.
Commitment	We ask students to reflect on their learning and commit to the use of this knowledge in their future reading and writing.

You use specific language to identify the parts of a unit and the parts of a lesson. How can I be sure I can follow along easily?

The language in this book is extremely user-friendly. We try to steer clear of jargon as much as we can. To best help teachers plan units and teach lessons, we have identified terms that help us all move forward easily. We have included a helpful Glossary of Terms for you on page 235.

What is the role of the Spotlight Units in the Complete Year books?

Each Complete Year book features eight bonus Spotlight Units, designed to help you understand what each unit of study can look and feel like in your classroom—both in terms of the concrete day-to-day details as well as the "learning energy" that you create through your instructional language and strategies. During the Spotlight Units, we invite you into our classrooms to sit by our sides and listen as we interact with our students. While we know you'll use your own language that reflects your unique teaching personality, we provide examples of language we use in our classrooms as a model for you to adapt. Learning how to craft our teaching language in artful ways that encourage active student participation takes practice; for example, knowing how to design open-ended questions rather than questions that just elicit a yes–no response is an art, typically learned through classroom-tested trial and error. Sometimes it's helpful to listen in on another teacher and notice how she uses language to frame each teaching moment.

Inside the Spotlight Units, you'll find one reading unit and one writing unit in each of the Complete 4 components (Process, Genre, Strategy, and Conventions). Our Spotlight Units also include unit templates, so you can see how we translate the templates into day-by-day lesson plans. You'll notice that not all bullets are translated directly into lessons and that the flow of the unit is fluid and flexible so you can adapt it in ways that fit your students' unique needs and interests.

How do I use the unit templates?

We envision teachers taking the templates we provide for each unit and adapting them to their students. Perhaps you have favorite books you love to read in your nonfiction unit. Or perhaps your students need more than one day on a bulleted lesson. While the templates offer guidelines for the overall structure of a unit and suggestions for how the unit might be paced, we see them as a road atlas, a guide that leads you toward your goal but also gives you the opportunity to add your own special touches along the way. Many teachers like to keep these unit templates on their desks as a reminder of where they are going, to help them plan each day's lesson.

How will I assess my students through the Complete Year?

The structure of the Complete 4 classroom gives you a rich opportunity to assess your students during their Independent Practice. Units of study give you regular, frequent opportunities to take stock of your students' progress. At the end of each unit is an assessment form for you to use.

Chapter 6 is dedicated to the C4 Assessment (C4A), a comprehensive tool designed for your grade level. You can use the C4A three times a year for both reading and writing. Quick and easy, the C4A will provide valuable information on your students' progress in all areas of reading and writing instruction.

The Complete Year in Grade 1

Our learning time with our students, bound by the parameters of the school year, is organized by seasons, so we thought it would be helpful to organize our books that way, too.

For first graders, the entry to this new year is brimming with excitement. They learned last year how to get around the school and how to manage the routines of recess and the bus. So now they are feeling like big kids coming back to school. And yet when they arrive on that first day, their first instinct is to grab on to you like a life raft. They have forgotten the intensity of the school day, and they get very tired by the end of it. They are eager to make the connection to their new classroom and to understand everything. That is simultaneously tiring and exhilarating. In late fall they have quickly incorporated your routines and internalized them. Yet on the playground there are whole other worlds simmering. You realize that this year will be a big one in terms of social growth and awareness, too.

In winter they are deeply immersed in their learning, proudly reading and writing. You help them to investigate the genre of nonfiction, and they feel like researchers and scientists, their heads firmly bent over pages of drafts and poring over pages of intriguing informational texts. Yet on other fronts, there are red flags. You see some of your students struggling with print and fluency. Take action at this time—do not wait. The red flags of winter in first grade tell a very important story.

With spring comes a new and exhilarating energy: your students can write in many genres and experiment with craft. They have absorbed the sound and magic of your read-alouds, and you see evidence of those influences directly in their writing. It is tremendously exciting. Late spring is a time of wonder and joy: poetry fills the air. Students' sentences in their written stories look cleaner and more conventional; they really can revise. There is celebration in the air—soon to become second graders, the students celebrate their developing skills. Yet they still want to hold your hand on the way to lunch.

Get ready now for the Complete Year experience. It is timely and timeless (and won't cost YOU time). Flexible and friendly (and fun). Easy to use and easy to navigate (and easy to explain to parents). Standards-based and field tested (in hundreds of classrooms). Made for you (to simplify your teaching life and to reconnect you with the joy of teaching). Made for your first graders (especially).

Have a great year!

Chapter 2

EARLY FALL

The First Grader as Thoughtful Choice Maker

"What is the seashore like?" a little boy asked his mother. He lived in the mountains and had never seen the sea. His mother smiled. "Let's pretend," she said. "It's early morning at the seashore and it's hard to tell where the sea stops and sky begins."

—from *The Seashore Book* by Charlotte Zolotow

Your first graders are brimming with questions. This season is about embracing their curiosity and imagination as they embark on a journey toward greater independence as readers and writers. Like the little boy in *The Seashore Book*, the first grader ventures into the world around him. Take a journey with us as we greet the new school year with units of study designed to embrace the excitement and energy of first graders.

EARLY FALL UNITS

SPOTLIGHT UNITS

EARLY FALL

LATE FALL

WINTER

SPRING

Beginning the Year With the ARCH

Our first units, known as the ARCH, are designed to bring our students together into a reading and writing community. This acronym stands for Assessment, Routines, Choice, and Healthy Community. The units balance the need to assess students as readers and writers with lessons on the routines of reading and writing time, the community-building aspects of reading and writing time, and how to make choices both in terms of topics and texts.

We must actively construct this community by establishing the daily routines for reading and writing time, discovering personal and shared interests, and introducing our students to our libraries and writing tools. Fountas and Pinnell (2000) remind us that during the first month of school you have two important goals: to help your students think of themselves as readers and to establish roles and routines. They remind us to repeat key lessons, chart the routines and roles of the reader and writer, and refer our students back to these points regularly.

As teachers, we are always a bit uncertain about how to begin the year in terms of content. We want to get to know our students, and we know we need to establish these routines, but we wonder what the content and outcomes are for this work. The ARCH is designed to blend both process and products: the beautiful work we do in coming together for the first time, as well as the important work we do in generating products that represent our students and move them forward at the very beginning of this school year's journey.

Each Complete 4 year begins with an ARCH unit at every grade level, but each year should feel different because of your students' changing developmental needs. (See page 112 of *The Complete 4 for Literacy* to see all the ARCH articulations for each grade level.) In first grade, our ARCH focus is Building Independence: Reading Role Models. In the reading and writing units that follow, we continue to build upon that theme with units that help our students discover the value of thinking and working across text.

The ARCH units set the foundation for the entire year. The ARCH incorporates teaching all of those routines and habits you long for and need when you are in the midst of your work with your students. If you set the stage now, you are guaranteed a happy, truly productive year of teaching reading and writing.

The ARCH: Building Independence: Reading Role Models

Why Teach This?

- To help students internalize routines of independent reading.
- To determine students' strengths and needs as the year begins.
- To create a supportive and trustful reading community.
- To help students see strengths in other readers and emulate them.

Framing Questions

- Whom do we admire as readers?
- How are we building a reading community?

Unit Goals

- Students will recognize the varied purposes for reading.
- Students will identify reading role models.
- Students will identify specific reading goals for the year.
- Students will make book choices that represent interest, level, and purpose.
- Students will share ideas when they read.
- Students will read independently for increasing periods of time (20 minutes by the end of the year).

Anchor Texts

- *All Pigs Are Beautiful* by Dick King-Smith
- *The Best Place to Read* by Debbie Bertram
- *A Book About Bears* by Mel Berger
- *Bread and Jam for Frances* by Russell Hoban
- *The Carrot Seed* by Ruth Krauss
- *Do Like Kyla* by Angela Johnson
- *In the Land of Words* by Eloise Greenfield
- *Inch by Inch* by Leo Lionni
- *Little Bear* by Else Minarik
- *Reading Makes You Feel Good* by Todd Parr
- *The Recess Queen* by Alexis O'Neill
- *Sophie and Sammy's Library Sleepover* by Judith Caseley
- *The Teeny Tiny Teacher* by Stephanie Calmenson
- "Under the Sunday Tree," in *Under the Sunday Tree* by Eloise Greenfield
- *Wild About Books* by Judy Sierra

Unit Assessment The ARCH: Building Independence: Reading Role Models			PROCESS
Student name:	EMERGING	DEVELOPING	INDEPENDENT
Follows routines of reading time.			
Makes book selections independently.			
Identifies personal reading goals.			
Works with a partner to share a book.			

Stage of the Unit	Focused Instruction You will	Independent Practice Students will
IMMERSION 6 days	• read *In the Land of Words* and share how words make us happy and make us think, tell stories, and bring people together. • read *Sophie and Sammy's Library Sleepover* and share how important it is to have a special place for books in the classroom. • read *Inch by Inch* and demonstrate using an egg timer to create boundaries and growing expectations for independent reading time (start small with two minutes, then move up to five, then ten, etc.). • demonstrate routines of reading time: whole class together, independent or partner reading, and whole class together again. • read "Under the Sunday Tree" and discuss the importance of special places; discuss successful reading spots within the classroom and at home. • invite guests to talk about their reading lives and goals.	• share with a partner a time when words made them happy. • tour together in partners the book baskets in your classroom library. • write about or draw a special reading memory and share with a partner. • practice increasing independent reading time with an egg timer. • make a goal sheet (either by drawing or writing) for how they want to grow as readers. • notice the qualities of reading role models by recording one thing they notice on an observation sheet or share with a partner.
IDENTIFICATION 7 days	• read *The Teeny Tiny Teacher* and name the importance of "one-inch voices" during reading time (quiet reading voices); name the importance of sitting in a "quiet bubble"; identify a regular time of day for reading. • read portions of *Little Bear* and *A Book About Bears* and model selecting books for interest and level in different genres. • identify goals we want to accomplish this year (reading longer books, reading for more minutes, reading about different things, reading in different genres).	• browse books independently or with partners. • identify behaviors that represent participation in a reading community. • practice reading in a "quiet bubble."

IDENTIFICATION *(continued)*	• read *Reading Makes You Feel Good* and make a list of why we read. • demonstrate qualities of a successful partnership (holding a book together, being friendly and supportive, allowing partner to read without interrupting). • identify terms for reading time ("turn and talk," Focused Instruction, Independent Practice, Wrap-Up). • read *The Carrot Seed* and talk about how we are all growing together as readers; identify what makes people strong as readers (their habits, environments, choices).	• select a book for interest and level and put in a book bag. • share a reading goal with a partner (I will read nonfiction; I will find a favorite series). • discuss with a partner why he or she reads. • discuss with a partner where readers read.
GUIDED PRACTICE 5 days	• read *Little Bear* and model kinds of things readers do during reading time (browse, read, talk, make reading plans); model daily routines; model one-inch voices and quiet bubble. • read *Bread and Jam for Frances* and demonstrate what readers do when they are finished with a book (reread, find a favorite part, share with partner, choose a new book from basket). • model what readers do when they share ideas about books (put a card on the sharing board, talk with partner). • model how readers share ideas about books; take turns when talking, listening, and reading; affirm a partner's ideas. • read *Wild About Books* and talk about how you will all be "wild" about books this year.	• practice daily routines and increase time on the egg timer. • practice what readers do when they are finished with a book. • collect books in a basket that represent different interests and levels. • practice sharing book ideas with others. • make a "wild about books" notecard and share one way they will try something new as readers.
COMMITMENT 2 days	• model goal setting (will read in many genres, will read for a certain number of minutes each day, will read for different purposes). • celebrate reading; name one person you admire as a reader and share why.	• draw or write a list of reading goals. • celebrate your reading role model by writing that person's name or drawing a picture of that person on a card and hanging it up in the room.
TOTAL: 20 DAYS		

The ARCH: Building Independence: Using Writing Role Models

Why Teach This?

- To help students recognize the routines of writing time.
- To determine students' strengths and needs as the year begins.
- To create participation in a writing community.
- To help students develop writing role models.

Framing Questions

- How are we developing a writing community?
- How are we using tools and materials to become writers?
- Whom do we admire as writers?

Unit Goals

- Students will understand and follow the routines of writing time.
- Students will generate writing ideas independently.
- Students will understand how to make choices regarding a variety of writing materials.
- Students will represent ideas through words.
- Students will identify writing role models.

Anchor Texts

- *Dear Annie* by Judith Caseley
- *Hair Dance!* by Dinah Johnson
- *My Map Book* by Sara Fanelli
- *The Racecar Alphabet* by Brian Floca
- *The Seashore Book* by Charlotte Zolotow
- *Under the Sunday Tree* by Eloise Greenfield
- *Voices of the Heart* by Ed Young

Unit Assessment The ARCH: Building Independence: Using Writing Role Models PROCESS			
Student name:	EMERGING	DEVELOPING	INDEPENDENT
Understands how to manage writing materials in a writing folder.			
Generates writing ideas from experiences and passions.			
Uses materials from the writing center to create writing.			
Creates stories using pictures and words.			
Writes independently for a sustained period of time.			

Stage of the Unit	Focused Instruction You will	Independent Practice Students will
IMMERSION 8 days	• read *My Map Book* and discuss how writing time will reflect what is in our hearts. • read *Under the Sunday Tree* and discuss where Eloise Greenfield found her inspiration; reflect on how you select writing ideas. • read *The Racecar Alphabet* and discuss how writers write about their passions. • read *Hair Dance!* and discuss how writers get ideas from their lives. • model how to establish routines of writing time (find a comfortable place, etc.). • reflect on whom you admire as a writer and why. • share your goals for writing this year. • demonstrate how you personalize your writing folder. • have students generate a baseline writing piece (a beginning-of-year writing sample).	• explore their own writing preferences by thinking, talking, and writing with others. • practice selecting writing ideas by writing about things that feel important to them. • practice routines of writing time. • talk about writing role models. • create a list of writing goals for themselves and share their writing goals with a partner. • personalize writing folders. • create a self-portrait with words and pictures. • write ideas; do a Welcome to My World picture chart; describe their passions, interests, and what their world feels like to them.
IDENTIFICATION 5 days	• show purposes for writing folder (for drafts and finished pieces). • model your own Welcome to My World chart. • read *The Seashore Book* and discuss how writers use all their senses to write about what they love. • read *Dear Annie* and demonstrate purposes for writing.	• share Welcome to My World charts and use them to generate writing ideas. • choose one picture book to look at while writing to inspire thinking. • use their senses as they write to convey things they love. • make a list to attach to folder of all the different kinds of writing there are in the world.
GUIDED PRACTICE 7 days	• read *Voices of the Heart* and model how writers are inspired by their passions. • model using a variety of writing paper (with lines, without lines, poetry paper, more lines, fewer lines). • demonstrate how you wonder, remember, observe, and imagine when you write.	• tell stories to one another. • practice selecting a variety of papers to write on. • keep an ongoing chart called What Our Writing Role Models Teach Us About Great Writing.

GUIDED PRACTICE *(continued)*	• demonstrate spelling strategies; model use of alphabet chart. • model working with a partner (knee to knee) to hear each other's stories. • model a writing conference and explain procedures. • model a story circle.	• practice writing what you wonder, remember, observe, and imagine. • take a piece of writing through the process from generating an idea to publishing. • share stories with one another, sitting knee to knee. • practice growing stronger as a storyteller by sitting in small circles and passing the "story stone" around, adding on to one another's stories.
COMMITMENT 2 days	• celebrate writing by having students read in small story circles. • name the qualities you admire in other writers and put up on a culminating chart.	• celebrate writing. • name the qualities they admire in other writers in the class; write compliments to writers in the class and hang them up on the wall.
TOTAL: 22 DAYS		

Students personalize their writing folders with images, words, art, and photos from their lives, which are reflective of their interests, passions, and experiences.

Print Matters

The first grader is ready to hit the ground running. He is hungry for print strategies, looking at his older siblings or the bigger kids around him as they navigate the world with bigger books in hand. The year has just begun, and he is ever so ready to play the game. It is time to learn to read. Let this year be a safety net for your students; if you see they are not acclimating to print early in the year, use all the resources in your school to provide students with the help they need. This year is an explosion into the world of language, print on the page, and print everywhere. These two units support your students' investigations. The print unit provides an overview of strategies for decoding difficult words. The writing unit presents a celebration of the ways writers communicate. They are making themselves known to the world through signs and letters. These kinds of writing are perfect for first graders who want to stand up and say, "Here I am!"

Developing Print Strategies

CONVENTIONS

Why Teach This?

- To help students become problem solvers as they read.
- To begin to understand some strategies to try when they come to a new word.
- To help students learn that reading is a meaning-making process.

Framing Questions

- What strategies can we try when we come to an unknown word?
- How do reading strategies help us when we are reading?
- Are we reading for meaning?

Unit Goals

- Students will learn strategies to use when they come to an unknown word.
- Students will practice using reading strategies in large and small groups.
- Students will understand that there is more than one way to decode an unknown word when they get to a tricky spot in their reading.

Anchor Texts

- Emergent Big Books or poems that can be used to show how to solve new words such as *Mrs. Wishy-Washy's Tub* by Joy Cowley and *Who's in the Tub?* by Sylvia M. Jones
- Independent book boxes with leveled books for children and other titles from a well-stocked classroom library
- *Snow Day!* by Lester Laminack

Unit Assessment Developing Print Strategies			CONVENTIONS
Student name:	EMERGING	DEVELOPING	INDEPENDENT
Has one-to-one match when reading print (can point to each word when reading, identifying each word as a separate entity).			
Understands that we read from left to right.			
Looks at the words when reading.			
Understands that print has meaning.			
Notices patterns in books.			
Gets mouth ready for the beginning sound of a word and checks the picture when encountering an unknown word.			
Tries multiple strategies when encountering an unknown word.			
Uses visual cues when reading (asks if it looks right).			
Uses structural cues when reading (asks if it sounds right).			
Uses meaning when he reads (asks if it makes sense).			

Stage of the Unit	Focused Instruction You will	Independent Practice Students will
IMMERSION 2 days	• read *Who's in the Tub?* and discuss that there are many strategies we can try when we come to an unknown word. • continue reading *Who's in the Tub?* and model how to take a picture walk through the text, moving from left to right through the print; share how you are thinking about print as you move through a text (assessment continues throughout the unit).	• practice looking at a book while moving from left to right. • take a picture walk in a new book, telling a story with the pictures only.

IDENTIFICATION
1 day
	• identify strategies on a chart, pointing out that readers use strategies such as the following to help them read:
	  • look at the words
	  • notice patterns
	  • get their mouths ready for the beginning sound and check the pictures
	  • ask, "Does it look right?"
	  • ask, "Does it sound right?"
	  • ask, "Does it make sense?"
		• browse books; practice reading from left to right; take a picture walk with a partner; begin to think about strategies they can use when they read.

GUIDED PRACTICE
6 days
	• read *Mrs. Wishy-Washy's Tub*, modeling what readers do when they come to an unknown word.
	• use *Mrs. Wishy-Washy's Tub* to model how to look at the words as you read.
	• model noticing patterns in books and explain how this helps us to read.
	• read *Snow Day!* and model getting your mouth ready and checking the picture when you come to an unknown word.
	• use *Snow Day!* to show students how to use the question, "Does it look right?" (does what I'm saying match the letters on the page?) and "Does it sound right?" (does what I'm saying sound like talking?).
	• show students how to use the question, "Does it make sense?" (does what I'm reading mean something?).
		• practice reading unknown words using reading strategies
		• practice looking closely at the words as they read with partners and in independent reading.
		• practice noticing patterns in books with partners and in independent reading.
		• practice getting their mouths ready and checking the picture when they come to an unknown word with partners and in independent reading.
		• practice asking the questions:
		  • Does it look right?
		  • Does it sound right?
		  • Does it make sense?
		• think about how to use the right strategy when encountering an unknown word.

COMMITMENT 1 day	• model how to decide which strategy to use when you get stuck on a new word by scanning the list to help.	• reflect on the strategies that are most helpful when encountering unknown words while reading.
TOTAL: 10 DAYS		

Conveying Messages: Signs and Letters

GENRE

Why Teach This?
- To help students understand that there are many different kinds of writing.
- To teach students that writing is purposeful and meaningful.
- To teach students there are many ways to convey a message.

Framing Questions
- What kinds of writing are in the world?
- How do I know the best way to convey my message?
- What are some of the different ways I can convey my message?

Unit Goals
- Students will learn about different kinds of writing.
- Students will learn how to convey a message in more than one way.
- Students will write signs, letters, notes, and lists.
- Students will understand that writing is purposeful and meaningful.

Anchor Texts
Anchor texts that show how there are different kinds of writing in the world, including:
- *A Book of Letters* by Ken Wilson-Max
- *Clarice Bean, That's Me* by Lauren Child
- *Click, Clack, Moo: Cows That Type* by Doreen Cronin
- *Dear Mrs. LaRue* by Mark Teague
- *I Read Signs* by Tana Hoban
- *With Love, Little Red Hen* by Alma Flor Ada

Unit Assessment Conveying Messages: Signs and Letters			GENRE
Student name:	EMERGING	DEVELOPING	INDEPENDENT
Understands there are many purposes for writing.			
Writes a sign that labels something in the classroom.			
Writes a letter to someone.			
Chooses the best way to convey a message.			

Stage of the Unit	Focused Instruction You will	Independent Practice Students will
IMMERSION 1 day	• look around the classroom and point out the different kinds of writing; read *Click, Clack, Moo: Cows That Type* and discuss how people use notes to communicate; reflect on places you have seen writing in school, at home, or in the world.	• work with a partner and discuss places they have seen writing and the different kinds of writing in the world.
IDENTIFICATION 1 day	• identify the types of writing in the world and chart together; read *I Read Signs* or *With Love, Little Red Hen* and select signs and letters to focus on during the unit.	• work with a partner and name some of the signs that could be made for the classroom; discuss people to whom they could write letters.
GUIDED PRACTICE 7 days	• model how to make a sign using big letters and pictures that support the words, and then chart kinds of signs to make for the classroom. • chart kinds of signs to make for the school. • chart kinds of signs to make for a home. • read *Dear Mrs. LaRue* and model the letter-writing format and the importance of having a purpose in a letter. • model writing a letter to someone far away. • model writing a letter to an author. • read *A Book of Letters* and model writing a letter to a friend in the school or in the classroom.	• make signs for the classroom, identifying the bathroom, clipboards, library, word wall, and so on. • make signs for the school, identifying the first-grade wing, cafeteria, principal's office, and so on. • make signs for their homes, identifying the bathroom, bedroom, kitchen sink, and so on. • practice the letter-writing format, including greeting, body, close, and signature. • write letters to someone far away. • write a letter to an author sharing favorite parts of his or her book or asking questions of the author. • write a letter to a friend in the school or in the classroom.
COMMITMENT 1 day	• discuss the different ways to convey a message.	• celebrate the signs and letters written over the last two weeks. • reflect on the best ways to convey a message.
TOTAL: 10 DAYS		

SPOTLIGHT on Process

- Making Wise Book Choices
- Making Choices as Writers: The Four Prompts

In my book *The Complete 4 for Literacy*, I explain in detail how process units are designed to build identity, capacities, collaboration, and responsibility. Although these form the foundations upon which readers and writers grow, because they are so intangible they often take a back seat in our instructional plans. A student's understanding of herself and the actions that move her forward as a reader and writer are all such an important part of her growth as a first grader. Establishing a strong understanding of processes now will help us to move forward smoothly, rather than having to grapple with management issues later in the year. Our explicit instructions for working with a partner give our students a structure for growing ideas and supporting one another. Lessons on building community will create a spirit of joy and collaboration that is indispensable in sustaining the atmosphere of safety and trust in your room. In these units, students learn how to develop the essential process skills of book selection based on their levels and interest, and, in a paired unit, the essential skill of topic selection also based on their level and interests in writing. These capacities are critical to establishing lifelong independence as readers and writers, and so we have created lessons that take our students through the experience of choice in a supported, layered approach.

For more information on process units, please see Chapter 2 of my book *The Complete 4 for Literacy*.

Pam Allyn

First Graders as Decision Makers

The two units that come next, Making Wise Book Choices and Making Choices as Writers: The Four Prompts, are integral to the year. They are both about supporting our students as choice makers—as readers and writers. In reading, book choice is a huge issue for first graders, as they learn about selecting books at their level and based on their interests. In writing, topic choice is also a huge issue—it's hard to face a blank page. Our students need ongoing support on the concept of choices—how readers and writers make them, scaffolding their independence as they enter new worlds.

The following unit is all about making wise book choices that allow our children to work consistently on the task of reading in ways they find comfortable and that are profoundly important: the wiser their book choice the more likely our students are to become avid readers.

In *New Essentials for Teaching Reading in Pre K–2* by Paula Moore and Anna Lyon (2005), the authors state, "Researchers theorize that one of the benefits of lots of reading is that students encounter the same common words in story after story, building a corpus of words that they can immediately recognize. The implication of this finding is that there needs to be substantial time during the school day for students to engage in the reading of continuous text at their level."

Making Wise Book Choices

PROCESS

Why Teach This?

- To teach students how to make choices as readers that will help them become stronger readers.
- To help students learn how to monitor their reading and recognize level books.
- To encourage students to become more independent as readers.

Framing Questions

- How can you tell if a book feels level, uphill, or downhill?
- What kinds of books should you read most of the time to become a stronger reader?
- What support systems are in place for our students to choose books wisely and become more independent as readers?

Unit Goals

- Students will learn how to make wise book choices.
- Students will learn how to manage and monitor books in a plastic book bag or box.
- Students will learn how making wise books choices will help them grow stronger as readers.

Anchor Texts

A classroom library filled with books in baskets that are easy for children to access; leveled books; books labeled by genre, author, and other categories; model texts at different levels for first graders such as:

- *Biscuit* by Alyssa Capucilli
- *Henry and Mudge* by Cynthia Rylant
- *Jambo Means Hello: Swahili Alphabet Book* by Muriel Feelings

Unit Assessment Making Wise Book Choices			PROCESS
Student name:	EMERGING	DEVELOPING	INDEPENDENT
Can identify a book that feels downhill.			
Can identify a book that feels level.			
Can identify a book that feels uphill.			
Understands that to get stronger as a reader he or she needs to read mostly level books.			
Chooses a variety of books for his or her box or plastic book bag that are mostly level.			

Stage of the Unit	Focused Instruction You will	Independent Practice Students will
IMMERSION 2 days	• model how to choose books that are interesting to you from the classroom library. • discuss how students make wise book choices (using last year's students or other models).	• choose a few books from the classroom library based on interest and browse through the books thinking about choice. • discuss how they choose books based on interest and name some of their favorites.
IDENTIFICATION 3 days	• read excerpts from *Jambo Means Hello, Biscuit,* and *Henry and Mudge*; name and define how a book can feel using the descriptions "uphill," "level," and "downhill" and make the analogy to riding a bike or walking around (see chart in unit). • model how to choose a "level" book • identify the difference between "level" and "downhill" book.	• read books from their independent book box or bag and find a book that feels uphill; reflect on why it feels uphill. • read books from their independent book box or bag and find a book that feels level; reflect on why it feels level. • read books from their independent book box or bag and find a book that feels downhill; reflect on why it feels downhill.
GUIDED PRACTICE 4 days	• demonstrate how students will identify their "level" books in the classroom library; guide students to the best places to find level books in the classroom library. • demonstrate how readers look at the title and think about their interest when picking a new book, using *Jambo Means Hello.*	• try finding books that are mostly level for their book box or bag; make sure that most of the books in their book box or bag feel level (eight of about ten books). • practice reading independently for a sustained period of time.

GUIDED PRACTICE *(continued)*	• demonstrate how readers flip through a book to determine whether it is a comfortable fit, using *Henry and Mudge*. • demonstrate how to preview a book by looking through the pictures.	• practice looking at the covers of books to help decide if the book interests them.
COMMITMENT 1 day	• reflect on making wise book choices, discussing how skilled readers choose mostly level books and change their books on a regular basis.	• reflect on whether books in boxes or bags are mostly level, including only one uphill and one downhill book; fill out a wise book choice reflection sheet and discuss with other students in the class.

TOTAL: 10 DAYS

Getting Started

In first grade, it is particularly important for children to read level books that feel comfortable and smooth. This unit is all about helping our students to read at their level. Therefore you must know their levels in order to guide them successfully. Assess your students diagnostically and continue to reassess them throughout the year.

Structures and Routines

During the whole-group lessons, children will be learning how to choose books independently. During Independent Practice, children will read from their book bags, practice their reading skills while using strategies, and talk about how independent reading has gone for them. Asking children to be reflective as readers is an extremely important part of helping them to understand how to become strong in their choices of books. The management of the classroom in this unit is extremely important and sometimes challenging, especially when our students are each reading their own books! Let's explore some of the challenges you may face so we can prepare you to address them.

Dear Parents,

We are beginning a unit in reading called "Making Wise Book Choices." The purpose of this unit is to help children to become better readers by learning how to choose books that feel comfortable to read independently. These books should have only one or two tricky spots. This helps children to become fluent and competent readers. They are also learning to read for meaning, as we always read first for meaning. It is important that when your child brings home books to read he or she practices retelling the book in sequence after reading. This will assure you that the books are right for your child. The content of this unit includes:

• thinking about what a comfortable book feels like

• learning how to choose books to read independently

• understanding how independent reading helps us get better as readers

• knowing that a comfortable book has only one or two tricky spots

• knowing that readers read fluently

• understand that we read for meaning first

Please let me know if you have any questions or if you are worried that the books coming home do not feel like a perfect fit. You will know this if your child is not eager to read them! That's usually the best rule of thumb.

Thank you for your support!

Above is a letter you can send to parents to help support their children's learning in this unit.

Predictable Problems	Possible Solutions
My students have trouble reading independently for a sustained period of time.	Start with an egg timer, telling children they are going to read for five minutes and add on to this time in increments each day. Your students will enjoy the challenge.
We do not have enough books in our classroom.	Remember that building a classroom library takes time! You may make copies of familiar poems and some self-made books to fill the children's book bags. There are inexpensive ways to get books, through Scholastic, your local library book sales, and the website Reading A–Z (www.readinga-z.com).
My students are not using their reading time well.	Begin with a management system that offers rewards. You can manage this system with a planning sheet (see below and in Resources). Ask parents or caregivers to look each day at the plan and see if children used their time well. Give out daily awards to students who are reading during reading time (using their time well) and doing so quietly. Remember, first graders are eager to please!
My students do not know how to choose new books.	Keep a laminated card inside students' book bags. On it, place stickers that match the boxes from which children can choose their books.
My students are always getting up to choose new books.	There are two ways of dealing with this problem. One is to have a book-swap day during which children are assigned times to change books. The other is to have individual reading plans for students to fill out, noting time spent reading. This keeps them accountable and keeps them reading during reading time, as they know you will be checking their plans.
My students do not know what to do during independent reading time.	Be explicit in your teaching. You will need to teach everything, including but not limited to: • how to sit when they read • how to turn the pages and treat books well • how to put books back in their box or book bag • how to fill out a reading plan • how to decide when they need new books • what to do if the timer is still going but they have read all their books (read them again) • how to use a quiet voice when reading

Teaching Materials

In order for children to learn how to make wise book choices, the classroom is set up so students have easy access to books. There are three structures that help to support our first-grade readers: a classroom library, a place for leveled reading books, and a place where children can keep their independent reading books.

The Classroom Library

One of the best ways to help children become enthusiastic readers is to create an environment where there are books for them to browse. Access is the key component for success in reading. Research has shown that children who grow up with easy access to books are more skillful readers and more likely to become lifelong readers. Students can look at illustrations even if they cannot read the words and have conversations with other children about their observations. An inviting classroom library helps to motivate children to become readers. Books in the library should represent a variety of genres, including nonfiction, fiction, and poetry. Books should be placed in baskets with the covers facing out in a way that encourages browsing. The baskets of books can be sorted by topics, genres, and authors.

Leveled Books

A section of the library has baskets of leveled books. In order to level a book, we look at the amount of print on a page, the number of words, the placement of the words and pictures, and the vocabulary in the book. For more information about leveling, Irene Fountas and Gay Su Pinnell have many books on this topic. They have created an A to Z system to level books. Many of our first-grade students come to us at level A or B, and the goal is to get them to level J or K by the end of the year.

Leveled books should comprise approximately 20 to 30 percent of your library. These books are meant for children to read independently, so you will need a wide variety. Children can choose from these books once they have learned how to make wise book choices during this unit. If you choose to use the A to Z leveling system, you may want to assign each letter a colored sticker to minimize competitive feelings about levels. Your first graders are young enough to quickly absorb your system. If you are positive and excited about their choices, they will not feel competitive with one another.

Independent Book Boxes or Plastic Book Bags

Your students should have boxes or plastic book bags for their independent books, or some container that will not break and is easy to maneuver. They need a place to keep their books that is convenient and easy for them to transport during independent reading time.

Independent Reading Books

Independent reading books are published by many companies, including Scholastic (www.scholastic.com), the Wright Group (www.wrightgroup.com), Rigby (rigby. harcourtachieve.com), Newbridge (www.newbridgeonline.com), Mondo (www.

Classroom library

Nonfiction bins

Leveled book bins

Independent book boxes

mondopub.com), and Dominie Press (www.plgcatalog.pearson.com). Many of these books are leveled according to Fountas and Pinnell's system, while some have their own leveling systems. If it is hard to get your hands on any of the books, there is a website called Reading A to Z (www.readinga-z.com) where you can find books to print out that are already leveled. You can also use poems and books that children have made themselves.

Stages of the Unit

Immersion
Students are introduced to leveled books and the classroom library. You will begin to get your students thinking about how readers make wise book choices and how these decisions affect them as readers. A parent letter will also go home at the beginning of this unit.

Identification
During these lessons, you will identify and define how to make wise book choices. Explain that some books are easier to read than others and that students need to read books they feel comfortable with.

Guided Practice
You are now ready to have your students make their book choices, while encouraging them to think about how these books feel to them during Independent Practice. Your lessons will guide them toward understanding why readers make the choices they make—both in terms of levels and in terms of interest.

Commitment
Students commit to recognizing how they know when books feel comfortable to them. They will share their book bags full of the books that represent their independent levels. If there are ten books in their bags, then eight of them should be level, one can be a challenge, and one can be an easy read. This balance fosters fluency and stamina.

Dear Parents,

At the end of each day, your child will be coming home with a reading plan. These are used during reading time while I meet with small groups of children. Your child's job is to read independently. Your child knows his or her responsibilities during this time and based on the mark on the plan (check, smile, or star), you and your child will have a good sense of whether they accomplished what was expected.

★ **excellent work** (filled out plan sheet and read during independent reading time)

☺ **good work** (finished but did not fill out plan sheet, forgot a name or the date, etc.)

✔ **did not use a 1-inch voice or use his or her time well**

Please look over the plan with your child each day. Your support will help us to accomplish more in the classroom and help your child to stay on task during independent reading time.

Thank you for your support!

Above is a letter you can send to parents to help support their children's learning in this unit.

Assessment

The best way to assess during this unit will be through conferences, and it will be extremely important to meet with your children during this time to monitor their book choices and be sure they have made comfortable choices. You will need to meet with your children on a one-to-one basis in order to see whether they are choosing level texts that match their reading needs.

How to Use the Lessons in the Spotlight Units

In every Spotlight Unit, we have scripted out each lesson: the Focused Instruction, the Independent Practice, and the Wrap-Up. Where you see italics, we have provided model language; you are free to use it as is, or you may prefer to adapt the language to suit your needs. For example if we mention a book we might read aloud to our class, but you have one you prefer, feel free to use that one instead. Or if we use a personal anecdote as a demonstration, you should replace it with one of your own. When there are no italics, the lesson plan includes guidelines of what you and the students could be doing at that point in the lesson. You will notice that there is always a balance of teacher talk and suggested actions.

Day-by-Day Lessons

DAY 1 Immersion

Focused Instruction

As readers we are always making choices. In our classroom library we have many books to choose from. Sometimes it is hard to decide what to choose. When I think about my own reading life, there are many kinds of books I like to read. When I go to choose books, I look at the picture on the cover and the title and think about whether the book is something I may be interested in.

- Show the cover of two or three books that you chose from the classroom library and explain why you chose those books.

Independent Practice

Your reading work today is to pick a few books from our classroom library that you would like to read or browse through. Look at the picture on the cover and the title to preview and decide whether it is a book that you are interested in reading.

- Have students choose a few books from the library they want to look at or read.

- Have students sit at a spot somewhere in the room and browse the books they have chosen.

- Walk around and confer with children, asking why they chose the books they did.

Wrap-Up

I noticed today that all of you selected different kinds of books. Some of you chose nonfiction books, and some of you chose fiction books. Turn to the person next to you and talk about one of the books you picked and why.

- Students turn and talk to the person next to them about one of their book choices.

Tomorrow we will think a little more about choosing books wisely.

DAY 2 Immersion

Focused Instruction

- Before today's lesson, you may want to invite two children from a second-grade class (from your class last year, if possible) to discuss how they choose books, and specifically how their selections vary under different circumstances: when they are with a friend (partner reading), when they are reading alone, when they are tired, when they are reading for school, and when they are reading for pleasure. Your goal for this day is to show the children there are many reasons we choose different kinds of books.

Yesterday we previewed and chose some books by looking at the cover picture and the title. Today we are going to talk to two of my friends from last year's class who will share with us how they make wise book choices.

- The two students then share their thoughts about making wise books choices.

Independent Practice

Your reading work today is to talk to a partner about the kinds of books you like to read, just like our visitors did. Make sure to mention some of your favorite books.

- Students talk with an assigned partner about the kinds of books they read and how they choose them.

Listen carefully to your partners while they are talking about making wise books choices. They may be able to give you some ideas that can help you when you need to choose books.

Wrap-Up

Let's make a chart of some of the ways we like to make book choices and the kinds of books we read.

Name	How I choose books	Some of my favorites
Jayden	I choose books by looking at the pictures before I pick them.	Dragon books and Froggy books
Zion	I choose books by looking at the words and seeing if I can read them.	Any nonfiction books with a lot of photos, especially the ones about animals and robots.
Michaela	I choose books that my mom has for me at home on my bookshelves.	I like books about princesses and books that have funny parts.

- This chart can be added to as time goes on during this unit. The goal is for children to think more about ways to make wise books choices.

DAY 3 Identification

Focused Instruction

For the last two days we have thought about how we like to choose books. Today we are going to begin to think about how to make really wise book choices so we can get better and better at reading as the year goes on. Reading can feel like riding a bike or walking. Sometimes you have to go uphill, sometimes you have to go downhill, and sometimes you are walking or riding and it is level. We can think about books in the same way.

Sometimes when we read a book, it feels a little bit like going up a hill on a bike or on foot. It is a little bit hard. When we are riding or walking and the ground is level, it feels smooth—not too easy or too hard. This is what a level book feels like. Sometimes we ride or walk downhill, and it feels really easy as you move faster with little effort. That is what an easy book feels like.

- Read excerpts from *Jambo Means Hello, Biscuit,* and *Henry and Mudge.* Stop during each reading to discuss whether the book is "uphill," "level," or "downhill."

Independent Practice

Your reading work today is to find a book in your box that feels a little uphill. You have to work pretty hard to get through it.

- Students look through their book boxes or plastic book bags. They will find a book that feels uphill and put a sticky note on that book.

Wrap-Up

As we can now tell, sometimes books do feel a little bit uphill. Sometimes the picture books that I have read for read-aloud feel a little bit uphill. They are books that we may still want to keep in our book box or bag to browse, looking mostly at pictures instead of reading all the words.

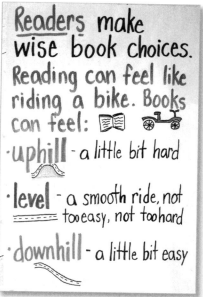

Sample chart.

DAY 4 Identification

Focused Instruction

Yesterday we found a book in our boxes that felt a little bit uphill. Today we are going to try and find the most important kind of book, the one we want to be reading most of the time. This kind of book is called a level book. Let's think again about riding our bike or walking on a level path. It feels like a smooth ride. This is what a level book feels like— you can read it without working too hard and without getting stuck too many times. You can also understand everything you are reading!

Independent Practice

Your reading work today is to read from your book box and put a sticky note on a book that feels level. Remember, this book will feel smooth and just right to read.

- Students will read from their book boxes and look for a book that feels level. They will concentrate on how the book feels when they read and whether they can understand everything that is happening in the book.

Bring the book that feels level for you to the Wrap-Up.

Wrap-Up

Turn to the person next to you on the rug. Show him or her the book that feels level for you. Explain what it is about this book that feels like a perfect read for you.

DAY 5 Identification

Focused Instruction

Yesterday we found books in our boxes that felt level. Today we are going to try to tell the difference between a level book and a downhill book. When you are riding or walking downhill, you have to stop yourself from going too fast. You have to put the brakes on and slow down. A downhill book feels like this too. You have to stop yourself from going too fast. A book like this is an easy read, but sometimes when I'm reading a real downhill book, I lose track of what the book is about because I can read it so fast.

Independent Practice

Your reading work today is to see whether you have any downhill books in your box. They may feel a little fast, a little bit easy. Put a sticky note on a book that feels downhill in your book box.

- Students look through their book boxes looking for books that feel downhill, an easy read.

Wrap-Up

- Students share out one or two books that feel downhill and what kind of read it is for them.

DAY 6 Guided Practice

Focused Instruction

We have spent the past few days thinking about the way books feel uphill, level, or downhill. For the next few days, we are going to spend some time in our classroom library and with our leveled books. We need to make sure that our boxes have a variety of kinds of books. Most of them need to feel level so we can read them and understand what is happening. Today I am going to give you a card that will stay in your book box. On that card you will see stickers with a color and a number. The color and number will tell where to look to choose most of your books.

- Your students will get an index card in their book box that has two stickers. If you choose to use a color system such as Red 1 for the A books, Red 2 for the B books, Red 3 for the C books, Blue 1 for the D books, and so on, these colored stickers will go on their cards. If a child can read a C book independently and well, you can give them a Red 2 and Red 3 sticker on their card. As the year continues, their stickers will change as the children become stronger readers.

Independent Practice

Your reading work today is to read from your book box. Some of you will work on making some new choices for your book boxes based on the book cards I will give you. The cards will have stickers to help you make wise book choices. Your box should have a total of about ten books. Eight books should feel level, one book can feel downhill and another can feel a bit uphill. The uphill and downhill books can come from anywhere in the library. The level books need to match the stickers on your book card.

- By breaking up the class into smaller groups, you can help to monitor book choice. This way, on Day 6 you are meeting with one-fourth of the class, on

Day 7 with another fourth of the class, and on so on. This way you can help support the children during Independent Practice as they make book choices. Although they are selecting from certain baskets, there are a variety of books in each basket and your support will help them to choose books that work best for each of them. This is a crucial time to help children make wise book choices independently.

Wrap-Up

By the end of the next four days, we will all have some wise book choices in our book boxes. From now on, we will always need to be thinking about making wise choices. Having smart choices in our boxes will help us to become better readers.

DAY 7 Guided Practice

Focused Instruction

Yesterday I met with some of you to support you as you made wise book choices. One thing that I do to help myself make wise book choices is look at the title to see if it is a title I can read and a book that I am interested in. Today I will continue to meet with some more of you to help support you to pick out some comfortable books.

- Demonstrate looking at the title and thinking about interest with *Jambo Means Hello.*

Independent Practice

Today I will meet with some of you to make book choices. The rest of you can read from your book boxes and think about some of the choices you have made or will make. Remember, looking at the title helps us as readers to decide if the books will feel comfortable and interesting.

- Students who are not meeting with you will read from their boxes.

Wrap-Up

Today we thought about how the title can help us make wise choices; tomorrow we will think about how browsing the book can also help us.

DAY 8 Guided Practice

Focused Instruction

Another thing that I do when I look at books to choose comfortable ones is to flip through the book and look at the number of words on the page and how many pictures there are. This helps me to think about whether the book will feel comfortable for me. If there are too many words I know it will be more of an uphill book. If there are too few words I know it will be more of a downhill book.

- Demonstrate flipping through *Henry and Mudge*, thinking about whether the book will be comfortable.

Independent Practice

Continue to read from your book boxes. For those of you who have already met with me, think about the books we chose and whether they feel level and comfortable. Remember, browsing through the pictures and the words can help us to make wise book choices.

- Meet with another fourth of the class, helping them to make choices.

Wrap-Up

Turn to the person next to you and share how browsing the books helped you to make choices.

DAY 9 Guided Practice

Focused Instruction

I also choose books based on what they look like. I like to look at the cover of the book; that helps me decide whether the book will be interesting to me. Looking at the pictures helps me to see what the book will be about—it is a preview of what is in the book.

Independent Practice

Today when you are reading, look at the picture on the cover; it will help you to see whether it is a book you might be interested in.

- Meet with the last fourth of the class, supporting them as they make wise book choices.

Wrap-Up

We have now all met together to choose books. Remember the things we thought about as we made our choices.

- Sample chart:

> We made wise book choices. Here is what we need to do when we choose books:
> - choose books that match the stickers on our book cards
> - look at the title and see if we can read it and it sounds interesting
> - preview the book by browsing; look at the amount of words and amount of pictures
> - look at the picture on the cover

DAY 10 Commitment

Focused Instruction

For the last few days we have been filling our book boxes with wise book choices, books that feel mostly level. We need to remember that first-grade readers read mostly level books, but also change the books in their box so we are always trying some new books. Today we are going to read during independent reading and instead of filling out our regular reading plan, we're going to fill out a plan that will help us check what kinds of books are in our box.

- Here is a sample plan that children can fill out:

Name _____

I have _____ books in my box that feel level.

I have _____ books in my box that feel uphill.

I have _____ books in my box that feel downhill.

I can tell that most of my books are level. YES or NO

Independent Practice

Today your reading work is to reflect on your books and notice whether they are level books that will help you grow stronger as a reader. After you look through your box, talk to a friend about the choices you've made.

- Use a student's book box to model for children how to take out the book card and count to see how many books match the stickers and how many are other kinds of books, either uphill or downhill.

- Students will take their book box and browse through their books, looking for which books match the stickers on their card and feel level and which books do not match the stickers and feel uphill or downhill.

- Students will rate the books on the plan sheet to make sure they have the right variety in their books.

Wrap-Up

- Students return to the meeting area with their reflection sheet and have a brief conversation with the person next to them about their reflections.

All of you were very reflective about your book choices. But our work on book choice is not finished today! You should be thinking about wise book choices throughout the school year, just as I think all the time before choosing a book. In our class you will choose new books about once a week. Each month we will use the reflection sheet again just to make sure we are on track with our book choices.

Boundless Idea Makers

In the late 1970s great minds in the field, such as Don Graves and Don Murray, broke through the tedium of years of unimaginative writing instruction with what felt like a radical concept: the belief that children have plenty of their own ideas and that going to the blank page was a lot more stimulating if children could choose their topic themselves. This understanding led to a true breakthrough in the field, and all across the country children began writing in writers' workshops, immersed in and engaged with ideas that came from their own life experiences. The hum and energy this brought to countless classrooms is immeasurably important.

Still, we have encountered many, many teachers who find those moments of blank-page frustration difficult to manage, in spite of the many good ideas educators have come up with over the years. It is not surprising, considering we have classrooms full of children with their own challenges, their own quirks, and their own reactions to the world of a blank page.

In response to this challenge, we have developed a very special unit of study called "The Four Prompts." The Four Prompts unit categorizes four major ways writers find ideas: wondering, remembering, imagining, and observing. Your students are still in charge of their ideas, and the passion they bring to story and to the blank page is all about what matters to them both personally and in relation to the world around them. But we have also provided them with the scaffolding that will help them get to that place of passion. And that is what the Four Prompts is all about: a secure and foundational way to build a set of ideas from which our students can draw the entire year.

Making Choices as Writers: The Four Prompts

PROCESS

Why Teach This?

- To help students think about different ways to get writing ideas.
- To give students a variety of writing ideas to choose from.
- To support students as writers, helping them to use the prompts to generate ideas.

Framing Questions

- How do writers find ideas for writing?
- How do we use our writing ideas to write with greater stamina?

Unit Goals

- Students will revisit favorite read-alouds and think about how the writers might have gotten their ideas.
- Students will practice generating writing ideas from the Four Prompts: I wonder, I remember, I imagine, I observe.
- Students will use their writing ideas to write with stamina.

Anchor Texts

- *Growing Frogs* by Vivian French and other Read and Wonder Series books (I wonder, I observe)
- *Mei-Mei Loves the Morning* by Margaret Halloway Tsubakiyama (I remember)
- *Night in the Country* by Cynthia Rylant (I observe)
- *Snowmen at Night* by Carolyn Buehner (I wonder, I imagine)
- *What If?* by Jonathan Shipton (I remember, I imagine)
- *Wilfred Gordon McDonald Partridge* by Mem Fox (I remember, I imagine)

Resource Sheets

- The Four Prompts and Our Ideas (Resource 2.1)
- Wondering Plan (Resource 2.2)
- Remembering Plan (Resource 2.3)
- Imagination Plan (Resource 2.4)
- Observation Plan (Resource 2.5)
- The Four Prompts Homework (Resource 2.6)
- The Four Prompts Unit Assessment (Resource 2.7)

Unit Assessment Making Choices as Writers: The Four Prompts			PROCESS
Student name:	EMERGING	DEVELOPING	INDEPENDENT
Looks at read-alouds and own writing to decide where ideas may have come from.			
Generates ideas from the prompt, "I wonder."			
Generates ideas from the prompt, "I remember."			
Generates ideas from the prompt, "I imagine."			
Generates ideas from the prompt, "I observe."			
Uses generated writing ideas to create a piece of writing.			

Stage of the Unit	Focused Instruction You will	Independent Practice Students will
IMMERSION 1 day	• read *What If?*; think aloud about where the author might have gotten his idea for the book.	• skim and scan familiar read-alouds and discuss where the writers may have gotten their ideas.
IDENTIFICATION 1 day	• name and define the Four Prompts (I wonder, I remember, I imagine, I observe). • model how to look back on a piece of writing and think about which prompt this writing idea could have come from.	• read through published and unpublished student writing, reflecting and recording what prompt each writing idea could have come from wondering, remembering, imagining, or observing.
GUIDED PRACTICE 6 days	• read *Growing Frogs* and discuss how authors find inspiration from wondering. • read *Mei-Mei Loves the Morning* and discuss how authors find inspiration from a memory. • read *Night in the Country*; model how an author could use observation as inspiration. • read *Snowmen at Night*; model how an author can use imagination as inspiration. • read *What If?*; model how authors can wonder and imagine to find inspiration. • model choosing some ideas.	• make a list on the wondering plan sheet of some wonderings. • make a list of memories on the memory plan sheet. • use their imaginations to generate writing ideas and record them on imagination plan sheet. • observe the world around them, using their senses to get ideas for writing. • choose some ideas from one or more of the Four Prompts and try writing off of the ideas. • try to add more to one of the pieces of writing.
COMMITMENT 2 days	• reflect on the writing from one of the Four Prompts. • choose one of the ideas you began and write off of the idea.	• reflect on their writing and choose one prompt to write more about and create a published piece of writing. • choose an idea from one of the Four Prompts.
TOTAL: 10 DAYS		

Getting Started

At this point in the year, you are beginning to notice significant changes in your first graders as readers and writers. They are taking leaps forward and are more aware of the world around them and the world of print. You have spent time reviewing classroom routines, assessing your students, teaching them about choice, and creating a healthy environment where they feel safe, secure, and willing to take risks in their learning. They are eager to please, ready to try new things, and feeling more comfortable as the fall settles in. It is a time of growth and opportunity.

Your students are beginning to write more and add more to their work. They are excited to share what they have written with others and tell the stories of their lives.

You may notice that some children in your class are overflowing with writing ideas. They are the ones who start new stories with ease and always know what to write next, and who will offer ideas to others in your class. But for some of our students, thinking of ideas to write about can be hard and often frustrating, as it is even for us as adults. This unit will help these students develop strategies for finding writing topics they care about and ways to continue even when they get stuck.

The Four Prompts unit is designed to help students develop ideas for writing that can be used throughout the year. The ideas children come up with are exciting and genuine, reflective of their growing sense of themselves and their emerging views of the world around them. Their ideas may be funny or innocent or surprisingly sophisticated. As you look through the ideas your children create, you'll find that rather than searching for ways to help them find writing ideas, you are inspired by the wealth of their ideas and how quickly they come.

Your students will be working independently during writing time to come up with ideas for their writing. It can also be helpful for children to have conversations with a writing partner. These conversations help generate ideas and create a comfortable writing community for students to work in throughout the year. Their wonderings, memories, imaginings, and observations are whimsical, funny, and interesting. They are the foundations for writing ideas all year long.

Structures and Routines

Students will work with graphic organizers based on the Four Prompts (I wonder, I remember, I imagine, I observe). If they complete the graphic organizer before writing time is over, they can go into their writing folders and do some independent writing, using their new thoughts to generate ideas. At the end of writing time, they will come back to the rug and share.

As you meet with each student in conferences you will gain knowledge and information about your individual learners, and you will also discover what you may need to focus on in future lessons. One of the best ways to manage this time is to use a box grid to keep notes. This helps you keep track of the children you have seen.

Tyrell	Anjoli	Michael	Kyle	Cynobia
Greg	Madison	Jayden	Henry	Carlos
Keira	Charlotte	Iyeoka	Superna	Heather
Aaron	Taro	Jack	Max	David
Nao	Lauren	Margarita	Kevin	Rashum

One way to make writing/conferring notes is to include the date, topic, what you notice, and what you have taught. There are many other ways to take notes as you confer with children. Try different ways and find out what works best for you. You know yourself and your children better than anyone else, so the best way is always what you are comfortable with and feels successful.

Teaching Materials

In this unit, we introduce the concept of the anchor text. This text is a book you will use over and over again as a reference during your lessons throughout the year. These texts help to reinforce the idea that writers have many ideas and write about a variety of topics. The chart below lists some anchor texts that you can use to support the Four Prompts unit.

Anchor Text	Author	Prompt Modeled (wondering, imagining, remembering, observing)
Alice the Fairy	David Shannon	imagining, wondering
Author: A True Story	Helen Lester	wondering, imagining, remembering
The Big Brown Box	Marisabina Russo	imagining
A Field Full of Horses	Peter Hansard	observing, wondering
Fireflies	Julie Brinckloe	remembering, observing
Growing Frogs and other Read and Wonder Series	Vivian French	wondering, observing
The Night I Followed the Dog	Nina Laden	imagining, wondering
Mei-Mei Loves the Morning	Margaret Halloway Tsubakiyama	remembering
Night in the Country	Cynthia Rylant	observing
Not a Box	Antoinette Portis	imagining
The Paperboy	Dav Pilkey	remembering, observing
Roller Coaster	Marla Frazee	remembering, observing
Snowmen at Night	Caralyn Buehner	wondering, imagining
Song and Dance Man	Karen Ackerman	remembering, imagining
Welcome, Precious	Nikki Grimes	remembering, observing
What If?	Jonathan Shipton	imagining, wondering
When I Was Five	Arthur Howard	remembering
Wilfred Gordon McDonald Partridge	Mem Fox	remembering, imagining

Other materials that you will use during this unit should include some of your own writing if possible. Be brave about this! Your first graders will adore hearing your wonderings, observations, memories, and imaginings.

Stages of the Unit

Immersion

Students will look at the many books we have read so far this year and think and talk about where writers get their ideas. By this time in early fall, we have read many books, sometimes two a day, from several genres. Therefore there should be a large selection from which to choose. You can also send a letter home to parents at this time.

Identification

This is a good time to look back at the writing our first graders have done so far. Although we have only had a month and a half of writing time, all of the students should have generated some writing by this point. Students will spend some time thinking about how they have come up with ideas for their own writing.

Guided Practice

We will be teaching children ways to generate ideas using the Four Prompts: I wonder, I remember, I imagine, and I observe. Children will be asked to focus on one of these each day, and they will work on of the graphic organizers accompanying this unit to support this work. During the Guided Practice, the modeling will be done through the anchor texts, teacher writing, and student writing. Students will use their writing time to generate ideas and work on their independent writing if they have time.

Commitment

Students will commit to this work by looking back at the generated ideas from the lists they have created throughout this unit and choosing one idea to work on to create a published piece of writing. They will choose a topic they can write a lot about and feel comfortable with. The rest of the topic ideas will stay in their writing folders as a tool to refer to throughout the year when they get stuck for ideas during writing time.

Dear Parents,

We are beginning a unit in writing called "The Four Prompts." The purpose of this unit is to develop new ideas for writing. The content of this unit includes:

- looking at familiar read-alouds and thinking about how the author may have gotten his or her ideas
- using the following prompts for writing

  I wonder…

  I remember…

  I observe…

  I imagine…

- thinking about each of the prompts in more detail and making topic lists for each

In order to support our work at home, feel free to use this language during reading and writing time with your child. Thank you for your support!

Warmly,

Above is a letter you can send to parents to help support their children's learning in this unit.

Day-by-Day Lessons

DAY 1 Immersion

Focused Instruction

Sometimes when we write a lot, it is hard to come up with new ideas. Writers can get their ideas in many different ways. We have spent a lot of time so far this year reading wonderful read-alouds. Today we are going to look through some of our favorites and think about how the writers may have gotten their ideas for the books.

- Read *What If?* and think aloud about where the author might have gotten his idea.

Independent Practice

Your writing work today is to look through the familiar read-aloud I have given you and your partner. Think about how the writer may have gotten his or her idea for the book.

- Students look at familiar read-alouds and put a sticky note with their thoughts on the front cover.

Wrap-Up

Who has something they would like to share today?

- Share sticky notes and chart ideas using our Author Observation Chart.

DAY 1	
Title of Book	How do we think the writer got his/her idea?
Night in the Country by Cynthia Rylant	observing, wondering

DAY 2 Identification

Focused Instruction

Yesterday we talked about how writers get their ideas. Today we are going to look at our own writing and think about how we got our ideas. This should help us to learn how we can get more ideas! Ideas can come from wondering, remembering, imagining, and observing. Where did some of your ideas come from?

Independent Practice

- Distribute The Four Prompts and Our Ideas (Resource 2.1).

Your writing work today is to look through some of your old writing or think back to some of the writing you may have done in kindergarten or when you were little. Think about how you got your ideas for some of the writing pieces. Write the titles or writing ideas you have used before under the prompt you used on the prompt plan.

- Students look through their writing folders or their published writing and write the titles or writing ideas they used under the prompt on the plan.

Wrap-Up

Look at your plan. Where did most of your writing ideas come from? Turn to the person next to you and share where most of your writing ideas came from.

DAY 3 Guided Practice

Focused Instruction

- Distribute the Wondering Plan (Resource 2.2).

Today we are going to think about our wonderings. Let's revisit the book Growing Frogs *by Vivian French. Maybe the author wondered about how to grow frogs, found out how, and wrote a book about it! Your writing work today is to think about some of the things that you wonder about. Write your wonderings on the Wondering Plan. This will help you later if you ever get stuck and need a writing idea.*

- Read from *Growing Frogs* and discuss how authors find inspiration from wondering.

Independent Practice

- Students work on filling in their Wondering Plan.

Wrap-Up

Today I noticed a lot of different wonderings. Julio wonders how a space shuttle goes so high, while Gregory wonders what teachers do in the teacher room. Devin wonders what children in other places do during the summer.

Our Prompt Ideas Chart		
Name of Child	Topic Idea	Prompt Used
Jennifer	zoo animals	observing
Tyreek	space aliens	imagining
Fatima	my grandma	remembering

DAY 4 Guided Practice

Focused Instruction

Today we are going to use the "I remember" prompt to get ideas for our writing. Let's think about our memories. Close your eyes and think about something that has happened to you. One memory I have is of my wedding. I could write a lot about it because I have a picture of the whole day in my mind. Think of a memory where you have a picture already in your mind. Turn and talk to the person next to you about your memory.

- Read *Wilfrid Gordon McDonald Partridge* and discuss how an author might find inspiration from a memory.

Independent Practice

- Distribute the Remembering Plan (Resource 2.3).

Your writing work today is to make a list of some of your memories. Use the Remembering Plan Sheet to write down your ideas. Your memories are thoughts about the past, about things that have happened to you that make you feel a certain way.

- Students work on their Remembering Plan.
- Confer with students, helping them to tell their memories.

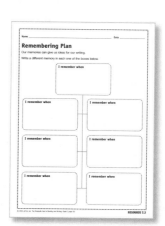

Wrap-Up

Today we thought about some of our memories. That is one way writers get ideas. Many of you have some wonderful memories of playing with your friends, spending time with your families, and doing special things. These are all things we can use as writing ideas.

DAY 5 Guided Practice

Focused Instruction

Another way writers find ideas is by using their imagination. Remember in the book Snowmen at Night *how the author used her imagination to think about what snowmen do at night? Remember the book* Alice the Fairy? *The little girl in the story has a big imagination and imagined what would happen if she were a fairy. Right now I want you to close your eyes and use your imagination. What do you see?*

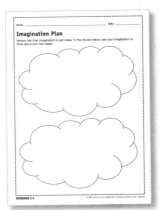

- Read *Snowmen at Night* to model how an author can use his imagination as inspiration.

Independent Practice

- Distribute the Imagination Plan (Resource 2.4).

Your writing work today is to use your imagination to help you think of a pretend story topic. Use the plan sheet to help grow your writing idea to make it even bigger.

- Students work on their Imagination Plan.

Wrap-Up

If we use our imagination, we can think of many amazing things. Turn to the person next to you and share something that you thought of using your imagination.

DAY 6 Guided Practice

Focused Instruction

Authors also come up with ideas for their pieces by observing what is happening right around them. Observation can be especially helpful if you are going to write a poem. We can observe through any of our senses. We hear things, smell things, touch things, taste things, and see things. Today we are going to work on making some observations about the world around us.

- Read *Night in the Country* to model how an author could use observation as an inspiration.

Independent Practice

- Distribute the Observation Plan (Resource 2.5).

Your writing work today is to use the observation sheet to notice things in our classroom and in the world (you can look out the window). We are going to put on our special pretend glasses that will help us see the world around us in a new and clearer way. Put on your special glasses to really think about the things you see. Then listen carefully to the sounds you hear. Open your nose to smell. This will help give us a lot of writing topic ideas. Use your Observation Plan to record your ideas.

- Students observe the classroom around them and fill out the Observation Plan.

- Confer with students, encouraging them to use their senses for this work.

Wrap-Up

We now have four new ways or prompts to help us find writing ideas whenever we get stuck this year during writing time.

DAY 7 Guided Practice

Focused Instruction

Over the last few days we have thought of many different ways to get writing ideas. We have thought about using our wonderings about the world as well as our memories, observations, and imagination. Today I am going to choose one of my ideas, a wondering about the world, and free-write (write as much as I can) for a few minutes, anything that comes to my mind about that idea.

Independent Practice

Your writing work today is to look through your Plan Sheets from the last four days. Think about which idea you feel most passionate about. Then use that topic idea to begin writing a story, poem, letter, or anything else. Your Plan Sheets are to help you so you don't have to worry about getting stuck for an idea anytime soon!

- Students look through all their Plan Sheets and pick a topic they are passionate about.
- Students begin to write on the topic they choose.

Wrap-Up

Today you selected one of your topics from the Plan Sheets. Turn to the person next to you and share what you wrote about and how the writing went for you.

DAY 8 Guided Practice

Focused Instruction

Yesterday we did some free-writing using one idea from our four Plan Sheets. Today we are going to do some more free-writing. Yesterday I picked one of my wonderings. Today I am going to look at my observations sheet. Hmm, I have on my observation sheet something about the snow and how it is glistening white. I think I will free-write a poem about snow! Turn to the person next to you and talk about topic ideas from your plan sheets.

Independent Practice

Your writing work today is to pick another topic idea and free-write. Write about whatever comes to mind about your topic and write as much as you can in the time we have for writing today.

- Students will pick a second topic from their plan sheets and free-write.

Wrap-Up

Today we picked another topic to write about. I noticed that many of you wanted to continue to write about your topics from yesterday. That is great. It means that you can write long and strong about your topic ideas. You can always go back to these ideas that you started and add more. That is what writers do.

- Send home the Four Prompts Homework (Resource 2.6).

DAY 9 Commitment

Focused Instruction

Today I am going to look back at my free-writes and see which one I want to make into a final piece to publish. The way to do this is by rereading to see which topic I feel I could write the most about, which one I could write about most easily. Writers choose topics they can write a lot about, topics they are passionate about, and topics that come easily to them when they try to write.

Independent Practice

Your writing work today is to pick the topic you think you can write a lot about. You may want to make it into a published piece to put your ideas and thoughts out into the world.

- Students pick one of the writing ideas that they feel they want to write more about.
- Students work on this piece during writing time.

Wrap-Up

Turn and share with the person next to you. What topic idea did you go back to? Why did you choose that topic idea to write about?

DAY 10 Commitment

Focused Instruction

Sometimes writers stick with a topic for a longer period of time so that they can get it ready to put out in the world for others to read. Today we are going to continue to work on our writing piece from yesterday so that it's finished and ready to put out into the world.

Independent Practice

Your writing work is to reread your writing from yesterday and add to it. The goal is to get these pieces ready to publish and celebrate!

- Students continue to work on getting their writing pieces ready to publish.

Wrap-Up

Over the last two weeks we came up with many ways to get writing ideas using the Four Prompts. This will help us for the rest of the school year if we ever get stuck as writers!

Conversations That Enrich and Inspire

First graders are capable of making deep and lasting friendships at this age, and yet they are also extraordinarily flexible and able to quickly adapt to new engagements with others. Let us use this new capacity for connection as well as their ongoing capacity for openness to new relationships to create structures for support in our rooms. We want our students to see one another as resources. As much as we feel a fondness for the little tugs for our attention and the smiles that go along with them, it is to our benefit and our children's to create structures that will support their independence and give us the opportunity to confer with individual students. Partnership units are critical at this time of the year: building foundations for multiple systems of support.

By studying the structures of effective partnerships, we create time to teach the process of effective conversations. Students can try out different ways of helping one another. Not only is this work great for developing their literacy, it is also an opportunity for you to nurture a values-based education—raising young men and women who from a very early age see the importance you place on discussion. It is an emphasis on collaboration, outcome-based negotiation, authentic support, and joyful engagement.

Becoming Strong Partners: Reading Together

PROCESS

Why Teach This?
- To help students become collaborative readers.
- To help deepen understanding of books.
- To support one another as readers.

Framing Questions
- How do reading partners work well together?
- How do partners support each other as readers?

Unit Goals
- Students will learn how to work collaboratively with a partner.
- Students will learn how to take turns and share books.

Anchor Texts
- *"Let's Get a Pup!" said Kate* by Bob Graham
- *Share and Take Turns* by Cheri J. Meiners and Meredith Johnson
- *Surprising Sharks* by Nicola Davis

Unit Assessment Becoming Strong Partners: Reading Together			PROCESS
Student name:	EMERGING	DEVELOPING	INDEPENDENT
Sits knee to knee and shoulder to shoulder with partner.			
Takes turns with partner.			
Uses a "one-inch voice" (very quiet voice) while reading with partner.			
Focuses on partner, not the others in the room (sits in a "quiet bubble" together).			
Shares one book with partner.			

Stage of the Unit	**Focused Instruction** You will	**Independent Practice** Students will
IMMERSION 1 day	• read *Surprising Sharks* with a student and demonstrate how to look at a book with a partner and share how reading together can help us enjoy books more.	• sit at a table with a partner and together look at a book from a basket on the table and then switch to another partner at another table and look at a second book.

IDENTIFICATION
1 day
	• name what strong partners do:
	  • sit knee to knee and shoulder to shoulder
	  • take turns
	  • use a "one-inch voice"
	  • look at one book together
	  • sit in a "quiet bubble"
	  • talk about the book
		• work on trying what strong partners do; name what parts of strong partnerships they did well and what aspect of strong partnerships they need to continue to practice.

GUIDED PRACTICE 3 days	• model how strong partners sit knee to knee and shoulder to shoulder. • model how partners take turns. • model how partners use a one-inch voice and sit in a quiet bubble together.	• practice what strong partners do (sitting knee to knee and shoulder to shoulder, taking turns, using a one-inch voice, looking at one book together, sitting in a quiet bubble). • try talking about the book with their partner.
COMMITMENT 1 day	• model how to reflect on partner work.	• reflect on how well they worked with their partner.
TOTAL: 6 DAYS		

Stop! Go! The Joys of Conventions

The following unit marks the end of the Four Prompts unit and, if you'll forgive the pun, "punctuates" the space between it and the next longer writing unit (Growing a Sense of Story: Writing Fiction). In this small lull between two major units, let's take some time with our students to study the rules writers use. Our students can practice with the writing they did in the Four Prompts unit and even publish a piece from that set of writing with a special attention to punctuation.

Understanding Rules Writers Use

CONVENTIONS

Why Teach This?

- To help students begin to reflect on conventions of writing.
- To teach students that for others to be able to read our writing, we need to have the following conventions: uppercase and lowercase letters, spacing, and punctuation at the end of sentences.
- To make children aware of these conventions in writing.

Framing Questions

- What conventions do we need in our writing to make it ready for others to read?
- When do we use uppercase letters and lowercase letters?
- How big are the spaces between our words?
- What goes at the end of a sentence so the reader knows where to stop or pause?

Unit Goals

- Students will learn that uppercase letters go at the beginning of a sentence.
- Students will learn that we use lowercase letters most of the time everywhere else.
- Students will learn to make finger spaces between their words.
- Students will learn how to put periods, question marks, or exclamation points at the end of a sentence.

Anchor Texts

- *Along Comes Jake* or *Move Over* by Joy Cowley
- *Oh, Brother!* by Nikki Grimes and Mike Benny
- *Smash! Crash!* by Jon Scieszka
- *Who's in the Shed?* by Brenda Parkes

Unit Assessment Understanding Rules Writers Use			CONVENTIONS
Student name:	EMERGING	DEVELOPING	INDEPENDENT
Uses uppercase letters for the word I, the beginning of sentences, and for names.			
Uses mostly lowercase letters where needed.			
Has spaces between words.			
Uses a period at the end of a sentence.			
Uses a question mark at the end of a question.			
Uses an exclamation point to show excitement at the end of a sentence.			

Stage of the Unit	**Focused Instruction** You will	**Independent Practice** Students will
IMMERSION 2 days	• read poems from *Oh, Brother!* and notice use of different conventions (spacing, punctuation, upper- and lowercase letters); ask students to come up to the book and place sticky notes on the places where they notice these conventions. • read *Smash! Crash!* and notice use of different conventions.	• work with a partner to look through familiar read-alouds and put sticky notes on places where they notice the use of writing conventions. • look through their independent book box or bags for books that model writing conventions.
IDENTIFICATION 1 day	• read *Along Came Jake*; name and define the following conventions of writing: uppercase letters, lowercase letters, spacing, periods, question marks, and exclamation points.	• look at their own published writing pieces, noting places where they used these conventions and places where they can add some.
GUIDED PRACTICE 6 days	• use *Who's in the Shed?*, children's writing, and/or teacher writing to model the use of writing conventions. • model the use of uppercase letters at the beginning of sentences for the word I and for a name. • model the use of lowercase letters as appropriate in writing.	• look at a published or unpublished piece of writing to check for uppercase letters at the beginning of sentences, at the beginning of a name, and with the word I. • look at a published or unpublished piece of writing and make sure most of the letters are lowercase.

GUIDED PRACTICE (continued)	• look through a piece of writing and make sure there are spaces between words; model how to do this. • create a piece of writing on chart paper that lacks ending punctuation and model how to fill in periods, question marks, and exclamation points. • read through a finished piece and check for conventions of writing.	• look at a published or unpublished piece of writing and check for spacing between words. • look at a published or unpublished piece of writing and check for periods at the end of sentences. • look at a published or unpublished piece of writing and check places to use a question mark at the end of a question. • look at a published or unpublished piece of writing and check places to use an exclamation point at the end of sentence to show excitement.
COMMITMENT 1 day	• reflect on a final piece of your writing or a child's writing, noting the places where the conventions are used correctly.	• celebrate a piece of writing where you tried all of the conventions; share with a small group; reflect on how this writing went.
TOTAL: 10 DAYS		

From Early Fall to Late Fall

Early fall has brought with it tremendous and rapid growth in your students' learning lives. Your year is in full swing. With the help of the Four Prompts, students will be making strong book choices and writing with a new sense of confidence and excitement. The role of conventions is growing and deepening in their learning lives. They have many new fundamental skills they will need in order to move forward in powerful ways as late fall arrives. Their worlds will be full of new collaborations in both reading and writing, and the room is alive with the sound of stories.

Chapter 3

LATE FALL

The First Grader as Builder of Story

"On rainy days, Olivia likes to go to the museum. She heads straight for her favorite picture. Olivia looks at it for a long time. What could she be thinking? But there is one painting Olivia just doesn't get. 'I could do that in about five minutes,' she says to her mother. As soon as she gets home she gives it a try."

—from *Olivia* by Ian Falconer

Like your first graders, Olivia is a builder, a creator, and a risk-taker. In this season, we will help our first graders build stamina and deepen their comprehension through collaborative opportunities. Join us in the following units of study, especially designed for first graders like Olivia who want to "give it a try."

LATE FALL UNITS

SPOTLIGHT UNITS

The Magic of Narrative: Imagined Universes

The two units featured next are predicated on the idea that story drives us as human beings and that children have powerful reasons to tell stories, to read them, to find universality in them, and to create their own. The preeminence of story as a foundation of thinking and of literacy development is a major theme throughout this book. First graders, with their toothless smiles and their dreams of the tooth fairy singing over their beds at night, live halfway between the world of fiction and the world of reality. These units seek to affirm the strength of story and the power of invention to propel us forward in literacy, as readers and writers. The entry point into independent literacy is the falling into story, the falling through the pages to the story, an experience your first graders will have as you read aloud to them, but now, perhaps for the first time, are going to experience independently. It is like Alice falling through the rabbit hole, or Lucy opening the wardrobe door in *The Lion, the Witch, and the Wardrobe* and feeling the cold bite of snow on her cheek—magic is there, and it is the door to new worlds.

Growing a Sense of Story: Reading Fiction

GENRE

Why Teach This?

- To help students become familiar with narrative text.
- To teach students about story elements.
- To expose children to retelling books using story elements.
- To deepen comprehension through understanding of narrative text and story elements.
- To use retelling as a tool to deepen comprehension.

Framing Questions

- What story elements can we identify in fiction?
- How does retelling using story elements help us to better understand our reading?

Unit Goals

- Students will have a basic understanding of fiction writing.
- Students will understand story elements.
- Students will be able to use retelling as a comprehension strategy.

Anchor Texts

- *Caps for Sale* by Esphyr Flobadkina
- *Elizabeti's Doll* by Stephanie Stuve-Bodeen
- *Froggy's Sleepover* and other Froggy books by Jonathan London
- *The Hatseller and the Monkeys* by Baba Wague Diakite
- *Lilly's Purple Plastic Purse* by Kevin Henkes
- *Owen* by Kevin Henkes

Unit Assessment Growing a Sense of Story: Reading Fiction			GENRE
Student name:	EMERGING	DEVELOPING	INDEPENDENT
Identifies the character(s) in a book.			
Identifies the setting in a book.			
Identifies the kickoff in a book.			
Describes the important events in a book.			
Describes the tie-up in a book.			
Understands how to retell a story using retelling language (title, characters, setting, kickoff event, events, tie-up).			
Retells a story using the important details only.			
Understands how retelling helps to support comprehension.			

Stage of the Unit	Focused Instruction You will	Independent Practice Students will
IMMERSION 2 days	• read *Elizabeti's Doll*, noticing story elements. • read *Owen*; think aloud, naming character, setting, kickoff event, other events, and the tie-up.	• browse through fiction read-alouds. • meet with partners and discuss some fiction story elements; place sticky notes in a book where they notice one of the elements of fiction stories.

IDENTIFICATION
1 day
	• use *Owen* or *Elizabeti's Doll* to identify and name elements of story using a story elements chart:
	  • character (people or animals in a story)
	  • setting (where the story takes place)
	  • kickoff (the beginning of the story)
	  • events (main things that happen after the kickoff)
	  • tie-up (how the story ends)
		• work with a partner to see if they can try to name one or more of the story elements while reading through a fiction book.

GUIDED PRACTICE 10 days	• model naming the main characters in a read-aloud. • read *The Hatseller*; model naming the setting. • read *Caps for Sale* and compare the settings of the two versions of this book (*Caps for Sale*, *The Hatseller*). • reread *Lilly's Purple Plastic Purse*; discuss the kickoff or initiating event and how it gets the book started. • reread *The Hatseller*; identify and name the main events in the book. • find the tie-up in *Lilly's Purple Plastic Purse* and discuss how it shows the story is over. • model retelling *Lilly's Purple Plastic Purse* using all of the story elements and a retelling bookmark. • continue retelling practice with *Froggy's Sleepover*.	• find the main character in independent books. • find the setting in independent books. • think about whether the setting changes over time and whether there is more than one setting in the book. • name the character and setting in independent books. • identify the initiating or kickoff event in a book. • identify three main events that happen after the kickoff. • identify the tie-up (the ending) in a book—what sums it all up. • use a retelling bookmark (a bookmark with pictures for each point of the retelling: character, setting, kickoff, events, tie-up) to retell the whole story in order. • practice using connecting language to retell a story (and then, or first, next, and last). • practice retelling story to a partner using connecting language.
COMMITMENT 2 days	• model how to celebrate retelling language using title, character, setting, kick-off, events, and tie-up. • reflect on retelling by modeling how it helps with comprehension.	• celebrate retelling by retelling a story to a small group using all retelling language (title, character, setting, kickoff, events, and tie-up). • reflect on their learning, considering how retelling helps them to better understand a book.
TOTAL: 15 DAYS		

Growing a Sense of Story: Writing Fiction

GENRE

Why Teach This?

- To make the connection between reading fiction and writing fiction.
- To strengthen comprehension of fiction stories by writing fiction stories.
- To create books using imagination and knowledge of narrative writing.
- To learn how to plan writing using graphic organizers.

Framing Questions

- How can knowledge of story elements and retelling help in writing strong fiction stories?
- How can graphic organizers help us plan for writing fiction?
- What are the story elements we need to include?

Unit Goals

- Students will use their knowledge of story elements and retelling to write fiction.
- Students will use graphic organizers to plan their writing.
- Students will create a piece of fiction writing.

Anchor Texts

- *Elizabeti's Doll* by Stephanie Stuve-Bodeen
- *Froggy's Sleepover* and other Froggy books by Jonathan London
- *The Hatseller and the Monkeys* by Baba Wague Diakite
- *Lilly's Purple Plastic Purse* by Kevin Henkes
- *Owen* by Kevin Henkes

Unit Assessment Growing a Sense of Story: Writing Fiction			GENRE
Student name:	EMERGING	DEVELOPING	INDEPENDENT
Uses a plan sheet to name characters and setting.			
Uses a plan sheet to identify a kickoff event.			
Uses a plan sheet to identify three events.			
Uses a plan sheet to identify a tie-up event.			
Uses a plan sheet to help write a fiction book.			
Understands the revision process for fiction and can make some changes.			
Uses an editing checklist to edit fiction story.			

Stage of the Unit	Focused Instruction You will	Independent Practice Students will
IMMERSION 2 days	• revisit narrative texts and name possible topics for narrative writing. • reread *Owen* or another narrative text and review the story elements (character, setting, events), naming them as you read.	• browse through fiction books and discuss the topics that writers choose for fiction. • browse through fiction books, noticing some of the characters, settings, and events.
IDENTIFICATION 1 day	• identify and name story elements to be included in a piece of fiction writing.	• work with a partner to name some possible writing topics for fiction by telling a story out loud.
GUIDED PRACTICE 14 days (Note: If students finish one fiction piece, they can start on a second one.)	• use *Elizabeti's Doll* and *Lilly's Purple Plastic Purse* to discuss characters in fiction and then list possible characters that could be in a fiction story for a class book; choose a character with students. • list possible settings for a class fiction book; choose the setting based on the characters (such as a giraffe in a zoo). • use characters and setting to discuss possible kickoff events for the whole-class book; choose an event. • discuss other events to follow the kickoff for the class book. • create a tie-up for the class book. • model good beginnings that get the reader's attention. • write a class story using the story elements chosen at the beginning of the Guided Practice. • model rereading to see if the class story makes sense. • model editing conventions.	• choose a character for the class story. • choose a setting that matches the character. • think of a kickoff event to get the class story started. • think of three events to follow the kickoff event. • think of a tie-up to make the story feel like it is over. • use their ideas to write their fiction piece. • work on writing a strong beginning that gets the reader's attention. • work on writing a middle that makes sense. • work on an ending or tie-up that makes the story feel like it is over. • think of a title that will get the reader's attention. • practice revising by reading to a partner to see whether the story makes sense. • practice editing using conventions so the story is ready to be read.
COMMITMENT 3 days	• publish class book and celebrate. • reflect on class book—does it include all of the story elements in order?	• celebrate writing, read their fiction to classmates (rotating with two groups over two days). • reflect on writing—does it include all of the story elements in order?

TOTAL: 20 DAYS

LATE FALL

WINTER

SPRING

Building Blocks of Understanding

The first grader is deep into the world of books, of print, of multilayered social worlds, of home. He is shifting more easily from one world to the other—more confident and assured. He is lively and curious as a reader; his interests are varied and sometimes eccentric. He may love his old passion, trucks, and also be newly interested in his big brother's passion, basketball. He may still keep his old bunny on his bed at home and even suck his thumb when he is tired, but he can run and jump and play for hours after school when given the opportunity. The time is ripe for delving deeper with our students into the strategies readers use to develop comprehension. The time is also ripe for developing collaborative structures that bring new energy to the classroom.

This season is infused with the theme of comprehension development, both through the collaborations and through close attention to story elements, particularly character. It is a ripe, rich time of year for your first graders. The following units are full of content for comprehension study and are a foundation for the reading and writing work students will be doing for the rest of their lives.

Making Meaning: Using Prediction to Further Our Thinking

STRATEGY

Why Teach This?

- To help students understand that if we use our prior knowledge, it will help us with our comprehension of stories.
- To teach children that making predictions about books also helps with comprehension.

Framing Questions

- How do readers use thinking strategies to improve comprehension?
- How does prior knowledge help us as readers?
- What does a wise book prediction sound like?

Unit Goals

- Students will use prior knowledge to make thoughtful predictions.
- Students will use their predictions to deepen comprehension.
- Students will use pictures, words, and character actions to become more thoughtful readers.

Anchor Texts

- *Anansi the Spider: A Tale from the Ashanti* by Gerald McDermott
- *Giraffes Can't Dance* by Giles Anderea
- *Hannah Duck* by Angie Yamamura
- *"Let's Get a Pup!" said Kate* by Bob Graham
- *Muncha! Muncha! Muncha!* by Candace Fleming
- *Tacky the Penguin* and other Tacky books by Helen Lester

Unit Assessment Making Meaning: Using Prediction to Further Our Thinking			STRATEGY
Student name:	EMERGING	DEVELOPING	INDEPENDENT
Uses prior knowledge as a place to start with prediction.			
Uses the cover and/or title to make smart predictions.			
Uses the words in the book to make smart predictions.			
Uses the pictures to make smart predictions.			
Thinks about character actions and character feelings to make smart predictions.			
Understands how prediction can help us with comprehension of text.			

Stage of the Unit	Focused Instruction You will	Independent Practice Students will
IMMERSION 1 day	• define the word *prediction* and what it means to make predictions in the real world. • model a real-world prediction about the weather.	• pay attention to themselves as readers and try predicting in their reading.
IDENTIFICATION 1 day	• name and define prediction again, this time focusing on what it means to make predictions in books.	• spy on themselves as readers and practice making smart predictions using what they already know about the world (prior knowledge); and put a sticky note on a place where they stopped to think.
GUIDED PRACTICE 8 days	• read *Muncha! Muncha! Muncha!* or *Hannah Duck* and model stopping to think aloud. • use *Muncha! Muncha! Muncha!* or *Hannah Duck* to model stopping to think with a "stop and think" bookmark, making the prediction and then reading on to prove it. • model making predictions using *Tacky the Penguin* or *Anansi the Spider*.	• work with a partner or independently to find a new book in the classroom each day, and practice predicting or stopping to think using the • title on the cover • pictures on the cover • title and pictures together • pictures in the book • words in the book • characters' feelings • characters' actions

GUIDED PRACTICE *(continued)*	• model making predictions using the title and pictures on the cover of *Tacky the Penguin* or *Anansi the Spider*. • read *Tacky the Penguin*; model using the pictures inside the book to make predictions. • model using just the words in *Tacky the Penguin* to make predictions. • read *Giraffes Can't Dance* and model how to think about characters' feelings to make predictions. • use *"Let's Get a Pup," said Kate* to think about character actions to make predictions.	
COMMITMENT 2 days	• reflect on how accurate your predictions were—did your predictions make sense; did they support your comprehension?	• discuss with a reading partner how their predictions went—did they make sense? • reflect on their predictions—what type of prediction was most helpful to them as readers?
TOTAL: 12 DAYS		

Writing Endurance

Midway through the year is a good time to refresh students' writing energy with a unit on how to write "longer and stronger." In process units such as this one, the focus is on how to refine and strengthen behaviors that will lead to lifelong writing. We will still publish writing and consider craft elements, but our lesson focus is on how to get down the page, how to sustain writing for more minutes in a day. Each of these skills is important, both for the writing our students do for pleasure and for the writing they will do because it is required. As with sports, we build muscles with practice. This unit is about building writing muscles.

It is fascinating to watch first graders at play both at home and at school. They are thoroughly savoring their abilities to play and to invent games that last for long stretches of time—across days or even weeks. Their stamina for play is high, and one idea easily builds upon another. Our goal is to create this same energy during writing time. The word "stamina" should represent a joyful push forward in literacy: to help our students build the same kind of sustaining power during their writing time that they experience in play.

Building Stamina: Writing Long and Strong

PROCESS

Why Teach This?

- To help students choose writing ideas they know a lot about.
- To teach students that writers stick with a writing topic for a period of time.
- To help students build writing stamina.

Framing Questions

- How do writers choose topics they can write a lot about?
- How do writers stick with one piece of writing for a period of time?

Unit Goals

- Students will choose a topic for writing they know a lot about.
- Students will work on a piece of writing for a period of time.
- Students will understand that to make our writing stronger we can write a lot of details about one thing.
- Students will build writing stamina.

Anchor Texts

- *Author: A True Story* by Helen Lester
- *How a Book Is Made* by Aliki
- *Nothing Ever Happens on 90th Street* by Roni Schotter
- *What Do Authors Do?* by Eileen Christelow

Unit Assessment Building Stamina: Writing Long and Strong			PROCESS
Student name:	EMERGING	DEVELOPING	INDEPENDENT
Chooses writing ideas.			
Stays with a writing topic for at least two days.			
Rereads writing to monitor for meaning.			
Adds to a piece of writing to make it more interesting for the reader.			
Tells a story aloud as a strategy for extending writing.			

Stage of the Unit	Focused Instruction You will	Independent Practice Students will
IMMERSION 1 day	• model through new or familiar read-alouds how an author writes a lot about one topic.	• skim and scan familiar read-alouds with a partner and discuss topic choice and how the writer wrote a lot about that one topic.
IDENTIFICATION 1 day	• read from *What Do Authors Do?* and discuss ways authors write "long and strong" about a topic: chart with students ways that they can write "long and strong" (choose a topic they know a lot about, tell a story out loud to add more words, reread to monitor for meaning, add more to their pictures, and add more to their words).	• read through published and unpublished student writing, reflecting on parts they could add to or change; decide on a new or old piece to use for this unit to build writing stamina.

GUIDED PRACTICE
7 days
	• model building writing stamina by taking a piece of your own writing and
	  • adding to your words
	  • adding to your pictures
	  • telling a story out loud to add more details
	  • rereading for meaning, making changes as you go
	  • adding a cover
	  • adding a title that gets the reader's attention
	  • checking for a beginning, middle, and ending
		• choose a piece of old writing to work on throughout this study or start a new piece of writing, building stamina by
		  • adding to their words
		  • adding to their pictures
		  • telling the story aloud to a partner to help them think of more to write
		  • rereading for meaning, making changes as they go
		  • adding a cover
		  • adding a title to get the reader's attention
		  • checking for a strong beginning, middle, and ending

COMMITMENT 1 day	• reflect on your writing stamina, how you worked on one piece of writing for a long period of time and made that writing strong.	• reflect and celebrate the writing they worked on for the last seven days, sharing with a small group.
TOTAL: 10 DAYS		

Talk That Furthers Thinking

Here we give our students some really good strategies for talk and for deepening conversation. These smaller units serve as energy builders and fortifiers for the longer units and for the big work our children will do inside them. Rather than hope our students will figure out how to talk together in a process unit, we can teach these skills explicitly. And we love the voices of our children! This unit celebrates them.

Becoming Strong Partners: Deepening Conversation

PROCESS

Why Teach This?

- To help students become collaborative readers.
- To help deepen their understanding of books.
- To support one another as readers.
- To use talk as a way to make meaning from text.

Framing Questions

- How do partners support each other as readers?
- In what ways can we talk about books together?

Unit Goals

- Students will learn how to have smart book talks.
- Students will learn how talking about books deepens comprehension.

Anchor Texts

- *For You Are a Kenyan Child* by Kelly Cunnane
- *Kitten's First Full Moon* by Kevin Henkes
- *The Recess Queen* by Alexis O'Neill
- *Robots* by Clive Gifford

Unit Assessment Becoming Strong Partners: Deepening Conversation			PROCESS
Student name:	EMERGING	DEVELOPING	INDEPENDENT
Talks with a partner about a favorite part of a book.			
Makes observations with a partner.			
Uses the pictures to generate talk.			
Generates talk and ideas by stopping and thinking.			
Talks about new concepts learned in a book.			

Stage of the Unit	Focused Instruction You will	Independent Practice Students will
IMMERSION 1 day	• read *Kitten's First Full Moon* and model how talking about a book helps us to better understand what is happening and helps us to enjoy the book more.	• work at a table with a partner and together look at a book chosen from a basket; notice one thing and generate talk based on the observation.

IDENTIFICATION
1 day
	• name partner talk strategies:
	  • We like the part when… because…
	  • We noticed…
	  • This picture made us think…
	  • We stopped and did some thinking when…
	  • We learned that…
		• sit with a partner and look at a book together, then find a part of the book they both like and talk about why.

GUIDED PRACTICE 3 days	• read *The Recess Queen* and model partner talk using the prompt "We noticed…" • read *For You Are a Kenyan Child* and model partner talk using the prompt "This picture made us think…" • read a section of the nonfiction book *The Robot* and model partner talk using the prompt, "We learned that…"	• practice what strong partners do to deepen comprehension. • try talking about books using talking prompts (one per day).
COMMITMENT 1 day	• model how to reflect on partner work.	• reflect on how well they worked with their partner and how well they talked about books.
TOTAL: 6 DAYS		

SPOTLIGHT on Strategy

- Investigating Character Traits in Series Books: Character Clubs
- Writing a New Series Book: Character Clubs

Strategy is thinking about what tools (physical or cognitive) we need and have available to understand and solve a problem, create a plan, and put it into action to solve the problem. The effective reader and writer and thinker asks: "What are the ways of looking at this problem others have successfully employed, and what tricks of the trade can I use?" We often spend time teaching different strategies separately (making connections or asking questions, for example) when the real challenge is how to help our children understand what type of strategy would be best to solve a particular problem, and then identifying the particular strategy to solve it. The strategies we use depend on our understanding of what is happening in that moment as we read and write and how that relates to the goal we are trying to achieve. By properly identifying the problem, we can use the right strategy to fix it.

In *Strategies That Work*, Stephanie Harvey and Anne Goudvis (2000) write,

"The term *strategic reading* refers to thinking about reading in ways that enhance learning and understanding. Researchers who explicitly taught students strategies for determining important ideas (Gallagher, 1986), drawing inferences (Hansen, 1981), and asking questions (Gavelek & Raphael, 1985) found that teaching these thinking/reading strategies improved students' overall comprehension of text. Research by Palincsar and Brown (1984), and Paris, Lipson, and Wixson (1983), however, suggests that it isn't enough for students simply to understand a given strategy. They must know when, why, and how to use it."

Watching the first grader build a block structure or create a play with friends, we see how strategic he can be. Strategy units are about helping our students build these powers of concentration, connections, and inquiry in their literacy work.

In first grade, our children are developing deep connections to a multitude of characters who guide them through text plots. Characters are concrete and a lot like them, so they can not only connect with them, but also ask questions, infer big ideas, and make predictions. We will take a close look at how we can help our students become more strategic in thinking about characters. For more information on strategy units for your primary readers and writers and how we can categorize strategies so as to teach them effectively, please see pages 73–79 in my book *The Complete 4 for Literacy*.

Pam Allyn

Collaborative Thinking

Characters in books can affect children in profound ways. They can motivate struggling readers to continue to read as they identify or become familiar with a character. They can entice more sophisticated readers into rereading texts, thereby building stamina and fluency. In kindergarten, we read the Alfie books. Across many books, Alfie has small adventures and takes good care of his sister. We also read the Frances books. Frances is feisty and a bit stubborn but always endearing and silly, too. Now, in first grade, our children are ready for more sustained, significant work with characters. They are ready to do the strategic work of thinking across books with recurring characters and developing some big ideas about them. They are ready to make inferences about characters and prove their points with evidence from books. And they are ready to take what they have learned about characters and plan their own writing about those characters using what they know.

Investigating Character Traits in Series Books: Character Clubs

STRATEGY

Why Teach This?
- To teach students how thinking deeply about characters can help with comprehension.
- To teach students the importance of collaborative work as readers.
- To teach students how character traits span across series books.

Framing Questions
- How can a study of characters in character clubs help us comprehend text?
- How do character traits carry across series books?

Unit Goals
- Students will identify main and secondary characters.
- Students will know and understand character traits.
- Students will learn to work well in collaborative groups.
- Students will learn how book talk about characters helps with comprehension.
- Students will understand how knowing a character can help predict his actions.

Anchor Texts
- Dragon books by Dav Pilkey
- Fluffy books by Kate McMullan
- Henry and Mudge books by Cynthia Rylant
- Olivia books by Ian Falconer (great for whole-class modeling)
- Poppleton books by Cynthia Rylant
- *We Are All Alike, We Are All Different* by Todd Parr

Resource Sheets
- Our Own Character Traits (Resource 3.1)
- Character Homework (Resource 3.2)
- Physical Traits: What Your Character Looks Like (Resource 3.3)

- Personality Trait Plan (Resource 3.4)
- Character Reading Homework (Resource 3.5)
- What Is Your Character Thinking? (Resource 3.6)
- Character Comparison: Main and Secondary Characters (Resource 3.7)
- Character Comparison: Main and You (Resource 3.8)
- Character Web (Resource 3.9)
- What We Have Learned (Resource 3.10)

Unit Assessment Investigating Character Traits in Series Books: Character Clubs			STRATEGY
Student name:	EMERGING	DEVELOPING	INDEPENDENT
Identifies main and secondary characters.			
Understands the term "character traits" and can name character traits in a series.			
Works collaboratively with a character club.			
Compares characters across a series.			
Understands a character's relation to plot.			
Understands the difference between physical and personality traits.			

Stage of the Unit	Focused Instruction You will	Independent Practice Students will
IMMERSION 2 days	• read an excerpt from *Olivia*; chart student observations about the character. • read an excerpt from *Olivia Forms a Band*; add new observations onto chart.	• browse through baskets of series books. • think about which characters they feel strongly about and may want to study over a period of time.
IDENTIFICATION 3 days	• identify character clubs based on student choice. • model personalizing a folder for character club (use Olivia as a model). • model browsing through books, continuing to study the character of Olivia, looking across texts.	• meet with character clubs for the first time. • make a shared folder for their group work with pictures of their character on the front of the folder. • read through books with their group, noticing things about their character.

GUIDED PRACTICE
9 days
	• discuss your own personality traits—what makes you special?
	• notice and discuss your physical traits—what do you look like on the outside?
	• using *Olivia*, discuss the physical traits of the main character.
	• using *Olivia*, discuss her personality traits, finding proof of the traits in the books.
	• using *Olivia*, discuss how reading many books across a series helps readers really know the character.
	• think about what we know about Olivia as a character and what she thinks about.
	• compare main and secondary characters in *Olivia*; create a chart comparing similarities and differences.
	• compare yourself to Olivia, charting the similarities and differences between you and Olivia.
	• create a character web for Olivia, including what you've learned about her as a character.
		• think about their own physical and personality traits and show proof of them
		• work in character clubs to study a character in a series and do the following:
		  • notice and discuss physical traits
		  • notice and discuss personality traits
		  • give examples from the text that illustrate the personality traits
		  • discuss what characters may be thinking
		  • compare main and secondary characters in a series
		  • compare themselves to the main character in the series
		  • create a character web that includes what they know about the main character

COMMITMENT 1 day	• reflect on everything you have learned about the main character and chart this knowledge.	• chart and name everything they know about the main character in their character club to prepare for creating a character series in writing.
TOTAL: 15 DAYS		

Getting Started

This study is designed to come midyear, a time when your students are more proficient at working together and engaging in book conversations. One of the goals of this unit is to teach children how to work in character clubs, refining and developing their capacity for talk, and building on one another's ideas. These are all important lifelong skills.

Structures and Routines

Children will work in groups of three or four, arranged heterogeneously, based on their character interests. Vulnerable readers take more time to reflect and notice things in the pictures, while stronger readers tend to look mostly at the print. They can then be a wonderful support for one another because they all have ideas to share.

Teaching Materials

The crucial ingredients for this unit are good books with strong characters that are age-appropriate for your first graders. At this time of year, you will have a wide variety of readers in your room. Books with strong characters tend to have more print and are for the stronger readers in your class. This is one of the reasons why the groupings in this unit are so important and need to be heterogeneous. Here are some series we recommend for a character unit:

Title of Series	Author	Fountas and Pinnell Text Level
Puppy Mudge	Cynthia Rylant	E
Biscuit	Alyssa Capucilli	F
Little Critter	Mercer Mayer	H
Dragon	Dav Pilkey	J
Henry and Mudge	Cynthia Rylant	J
Poppleton	Cynthia Rylant	J
Mr. Putter and Tabby	Cynthia Rylant	J
Fluffy	Kate McMullan	K
Frog and Toad	Arnold Lobel	K
Little Bill	Bill Cosby	K
Nate the Great	Marc Simont	K

For this unit, students keep a pocket folder for their group work. They use this folder to store their work throughout the three-week unit of study and they decorate it with the name and picture of the character they are about to spend time getting to know. This helps create a sense of both ownership and excitement. Each group will have a basket for the books they will use throughout the unit. Have them keep the books and the folder together in the character basket, which they can easily move to their group meeting areas around the classroom.

Stages of the Unit

Immersion

Students will take some time to browse through the different series, noticing aspects of the characters, and then think about which one seems most interesting to them. Then they can fill out a preference sheet to tell which character they would like to study. You will then form the groups based on students' interests and choices. Try to make the groups as heterogeneous as possible.

This is the time to send home the parent letter to inform families of the upcoming unit and give them ways they can support your work at home.

Dear Parents,

We are beginning our reading unit on looking deeply at characters in fiction. The purpose of this unit is to help children think about the characters in a book and learn how authors demonstrate character traits through the characters' actions. The content of this unit includes:

- identifying main and secondary characters
- knowing and understanding character traits
- understanding the difference between how a character looks on the outside and how he or she behaves
- knowing a character well enough to predict how he or she would behave in certain situations
- learning how a character deals with problems

In order to support this work, please talk about the characters you find in books. Ask your children questions about the characters' traits, actions, and problems.

Warmly,

Above is a letter you can send to parents to help support their children's learning in this unit.

Identification

During the Identification stage, students are not yet in their character clubs. Students get their work folders ready and personalized and begin to browse the books together. Students will now be asked to focus their attention on the specific characters in the series.

Guided Practice

Students think about themselves and name their own personality traits. Then they choose a character in a series and notice his or her traits (physical attributes and personality) and compare the character to themselves and other characters in the story.

Commitment

It is time to come up with topics and ideas for a new book students will add to a series that they have been reading. For example, students who'd been studying Poppleton decided they were going to write a book titled *Poppleton Goes to School*. The Frog and Toad group decided to write a new book for that series called *Where's Toad?* This will lead them directly into the writing unit that follows this study.

Day-by-Day Lessons

DAY 1 Immersion

Focused Instruction

Today we are going to begin a reading unit called Investigating Character Traits in Series Books: Character Clubs. In this unit we are going to look at characters in series books with special detective eyes and think about how the characters look and act. We will learn their personality traits and think about how the characters' behaviors help us to better understand our reading. Remember the book Olivia by Ian Falconer? Let's revisit this book together. Think about some of the things you notice about Olivia as a character. Turn and talk to the person next to you.

- Chart some of the student observations.

Independent Practice

Your reading work today is to look at the basket of books on your table and think about the characters in those books. You will have some time to look through the basket and when the bell rings you can move to the next table and look through another basket. You will look through three of the character baskets today. While you are looking, think about which character you may want to focus on for this study.

- Students browse character baskets until the bell rings and then move to the next table.

Wrap-Up

Today we looked at three of the six character baskets with specific characters. While you were browsing, you thought about which of the series was your favorite and why. Keep that information in your head because tomorrow you will look at even more baskets.

DAY 2 Immersion

Focused Instruction

Remember Olivia and how we thought about what we noticed about her? (Refer to chart from Day 1.) *Today we are going to revisit another Olivia book, called* Olivia Forms a Band. *Let's think about Olivia in yesterday's book and Olivia in this book. What do you notice is the same? What do you notice is different? Turn and talk to the person next to you about Olivia.*

- Chart any new observations about Olivia, adding to yesterday's work.

Independent Practice

Your reading work today is to continue to browse the character baskets. Today you will look at the ones you did not see yesterday. Remember to think about which characters you are really passionate about since you will have to choose one character.

- Students continue to browse character baskets.

Wrap-Up

Now that you have looked at all of the character choices, please think about your three favorite characters. Put them in the order you'd most like to study them. You will get one of your choices for the study groups, but maybe not your first choice.

- This is a sample character club choice sheet:

Name _____

Character Club Choices

Poppleton   Frog   Fluffy   Dragon   Mr. Putter   Henry

My top three choices:
First Choice _____
Second Choice _____
Third Choice_____

DAY 3 Identification

Focused Instruction

- Assign groups based on choice sheets and knowledge of which students work together. Try to make the groups as heterogeneous as possible.

Today we are going to meet with our character clubs for the first time! In your character basket there is a pocket folder with the name of your character on the front. Today we are going to look at our characters and personalize our folders. Our folders will be the place where we keep all of our character work for the next two weeks. When you decorate your folder, make sure it shows the character you will be studying.

Independent Practice

Your reading work today is to decorate your group folder to represent the character you will be studying. Remember to discuss with your group your plans for illustrating and to take turns.

- Students plan and personalize their writing folders.

Wrap-Up

Today we made our work folders for our character clubs. Turn to the group next to you and tell them about your folder and why you chose to illustrate it the way you did.

DAY 4 Identification

Focused Instruction

We are ready to begin to read the books in our baskets so that we can learn about the character we are studying. But first we will revisit the Olivia books and, as a class, study her character. Our job is to really think about who Olivia is, both on the inside and on the outside.

- Discuss some of Olivia's character traits as a whole class.

Independent Practice

Your reading work today is to read one of the stories in your character baskets. Work with someone in your group or as a whole group to read one of the stories. Don't worry if you do not finish; we will have more time to do this tomorrow and will continue this work throughout the next few weeks.

- Students read one or more of the stories in their character baskets.

Wrap-Up

Today we read one of the books in our character baskets. Turn to the group next to you and tell them some of the things that you noticed about your character or something about the book you read.

DAY 5 Identification

Focused Instruction

Today we are going to continue to think about Olivia. What do you notice about her? What is the same about her throughout all of the Olivia books?

Independent Practice

We are going to continue to read though our character baskets today. Look for traits of your characters that carry over throughout all of the books in the series.

Wrap-Up

Turn to the group next to you and talk about some of the things you have noticed about the characters in your series.

DAY 6 Guided Practice

Focused Instruction

Just like characters in stories, people have traits. When I think about myself, I know that I am very sensitive. When I watch shows on TV I sometimes cry— sometimes even at commercials. This is proof that I am sensitive. Now think about yourself. What are some of your personality traits? Turn to the person next to you and tell them something about your own personality.

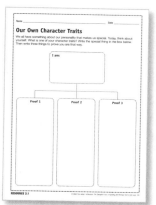

Independent Practice

- Distribute Our Own Character Traits (Resource 3.1).

Your reading work today is to think about yourself and one of your personality traits. Then think of three proofs that this is one of your traits.

- Students think about their own personality traits and use the graphic organizer to record their work.

Wrap-Up

We all thought about something that makes us special. Find someone from a different character club and tell them about your character trait. Remember to tell them how you proved that you have this trait.

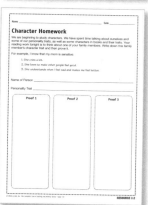

- Send home the Character Homework (Resource 3.2).

DAY 7 Guided Practice

Focused Instruction

Today we are going to think about ourselves as characters again. What do we look like on the outside? How is the way we look different from the way others around us look? We are going to think about our physical traits, like our hair color, eye color, skin color, and other things about the way we look. For example, my hair is brown and my eyes are brown. My hair is about medium length. After we think about our physical traits, we are going to do a fun project.

- A good book to read about differing physical traits is *We Are All Alike, We Are All Different* by Todd Parr.

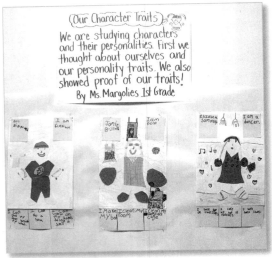

Independent Practice

Your work today is to draw yourself on the small cutout person (see photo at left) and then decorate him or her. At the top, write your personality trait and your proof of that trait from the sheet we worked on yesterday.

Wrap-Up

Now that we have made our own characters, it will be easier to think about the characters in our book. Tomorrow we will begin to look deeply at the characters in our character clubs.

- This project is a fun way for children to explore and illustrate their own character traits. It may take more than one day to complete, so it is okay to push back your lessons if necessary. The children will refer back to this when thinking about the traits of characters in books.

DAY 8 Guided Practice

Focused Instruction

As we discussed before, the physical traits of a character are the things that describe how the character looks on the outside. Let's think about Olivia first. What do we notice about Olivia? What does she look like? What are her physical traits?

- Chart the responses that children give about Olivia.

Independent Practice

- Distribute Physical Traits: What Your Character Looks Like (Resource 3.3).

Your reading work today is to look at some of the books that feature your character. Notice the physical traits of your character, what he or she looks like on the outside. Work together with the members of your group to draw your character and label his or her physical traits (what the character looks like on the outside).

- Students will work together to draw a picture of their character and label the parts they draw.

Wrap-Up

Turn to the group next to you and share the picture of your character. See if you can find some similarities or differences between your character and the other group's character.

- Chart observations of similarities and differences between the different groups.

- Here is an example of a chart created by our class when comparing physical traits:

Name of Study Group	Some of their Physical Traits	Similarities to Other Characters
Toad	a toad, black eyes, wears clothes, has green legs	an animal who wears clothes
Fluffy	a guinea pig, fuzzy, brown	an animal
Poppleton	a pig, pink, always has on a new outfit, fat	an animal who wears clothes like Toad

DAY 9 Guided Practice

Focused Instruction

Yesterday we studied our characters' physical traits. Today we will think about their personality traits. Last week we thought about our own personality traits and showed proof of them, so we are now ready to think about our characters' personality traits. Remember how Julia said she was shy, and her proofs were that she gets nervous when she meets new people, she talks quietly, and she used to hide under the table when she was little? A personality trait is how someone acts, something special about that person. Let's go back to our Olivia books. What is something that we know about Olivia's personality? What is something that makes Olivia special? What makes Olivia Olivia?

- Chart with students some of Olivia's personality traits with proof of each one.

Olivia's Character Traits	Proof 1	Proof 2	Proof 3
imaginative	She pretends to be a band leader.	She always makes up stories in her head.	She pretends she is in the circus.

Independent Practice

- Distribute the Personality Trait Plan (Resource 3.4).

Your reading work today is to think of some character traits for your character. Try to think of at least two traits and record your information on the trait sheet. If your group is studying Poppleton, then you and your group need to think of some of Poppleton's traits. Remember to use the book to help you. You will need to prove the traits, just like we did with ourselves earlier this week.

- Students reread and discuss the personality traits of their characters.
- Students chart the characters' traits and proof for each one.

Wrap-Up

Now we have all thought of some traits for our characters. Share one of the traits with another group. Tomorrow we will continue this work and try to think of some other traits for our characters.

DAY 10 Guided Practice

Focused Instruction

What are some more traits that make Olivia special? What is proof of these personality traits?

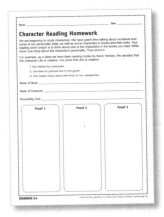

- Add traits to chart

Independent Practice

Try to think about another trait for your character. Make sure you can show proof of the trait.

- Children may be working on their second or third personality trait sheet with proof from the books.

Wrap-Up

- Chart student observations relating to both physical and personality traits looking across characters.
- Send home the Character Reading Homework (Resource 3.5).
- Chart for Days 8–10:

Name of Character	Physical Traits	Personality Traits	Proof of Personality Traits
Olivia	• She is a pig. • She is pink. • She has a snout. • She is small.	• silly	She tries on makeup.
		• imaginative	She pretends she is in a band.
		• gets upset easily	She gets angry at her mom.

DAY 11 Guided Practice

Focused Instruction

Once we get to know a character, we can begin to think about the kinds of things that the character may be thinking. For example we know Olivia is very imaginative. One thing that Olivia probably does is make up stories in her head. She may be thinking that she could be the president. She may be thinking that she is a scientist who discovers dinosaurs. The reason we know this about Olivia is that we know she has a good imagination, and we have read several of her books. When we read a lot of books about the same character, it helps us to know the character even better.

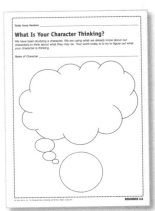

Independent Practice

- Distribute the What Is Your Character Thinking? sheet (Resource 3.6).

Your reading work today is to use the What Is Your Character Thinking? sheet to write down some things that your character may be thinking. You can each fill out your own sheet with character thoughts. Make sure to discuss your thoughts with your group members so that you come up with some different ideas about different traits.

- Students can work alone or in pairs within their group to record what their character may be thinking, based on what they now know about their character.
- Confer with students, helping them to think about their characters' thoughts.

Wrap-Up

Turn to the person next to you and share what you think your character may be thinking. Remember to share why you think your character could be thinking this.

DAY 12 Guided Practice

Focused Instruction

All of the books we are reading have main characters (the one we are studying) and secondary characters, who are other characters in the book.

- Main and secondary characters are familiar to children from our unit on story elements from the fall. They may need some review.

In the Olivia books, the main character is Olivia. The secondary characters are her mom and her two little brothers. Take a minute to meet with your group here on the rug and talk about who the main and secondary characters are in your series.

- Chart discussion after the children finish talking.

Name of Series	Main Character (the one we are studying)	Secondary Characters (other characters in the books)
Frog and Toad	Frog	Toad
Poppleton	Poppleton	Cherry Sue, Filmore
Mr. Putter and Tabby	Mr. Putter	Tabby, Mrs. Teaberry, Zeke
Henry and Mudge	Henry	Mudge, Henry's mom, Henry's dad

Today we are going to think about the similarities and differences between the main and secondary characters. Let's try this with Olivia.

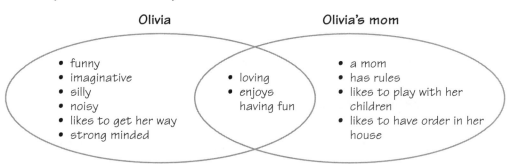

Olivia

Olivia's mom

- funny
- imaginative
- silly
- noisy
- likes to get her way
- strong minded

- loving
- enjoys having fun

- a mom
- has rules
- likes to play with her children
- likes to have order in her house

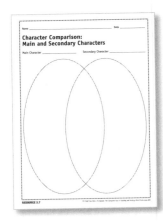

Independent Practice

- Distribute Character Comparison: Main and Secondary Characters (Resource 3.7).

Your reading work today is to think about the main character and one secondary character. As a group, think about how the main character and the secondary character are the same and how they are different. Work together with your group to name these similarities and differences and record your work on the Character Comparison sheet.

- Students will compare main and secondary characters from their books on the main and secondary character plan sheets.

Wrap-Up

Today we compared the main character to another character in our series. Turn to another group and share some of the things you thought were the same and some things you thought were different about the two characters in your series.

DAY 13 Guided Practice

Focused Instruction

Yesterday we compared the main character to a secondary character in our series. Today we are going to compare the main character to ourselves. Think about how you are like your main character and ways in which you are different. Let's try it with Olivia and me.

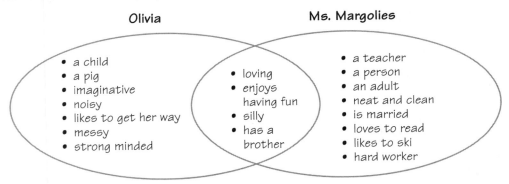

Olivia — Ms. Margolies

- a child
- a pig
- imaginative
- noisy
- likes to get her way
- messy
- strong minded

- loving
- enjoys having fun
- silly
- has a brother

- a teacher
- a person
- an adult
- neat and clean
- is married
- loves to read
- likes to ski
- hard worker

As we can see, even though Olivia and I are very different, there are still some things we have in common.

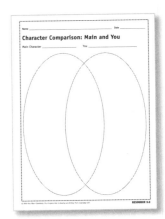

Independent Practice

- Distribute Character Comparison: Main and You (Resource 3.8).

Your reading work today is to think about your character and yourself. Using the diagram sheet, list the things about the character from your book first, then list the things you know about yourself and see if you can find any things that you have in common with your character. You will be sitting with your groups for this but working on your own during this activity.

- Each student will work on a comparison sheet, comparing themselves to the main characters in their study groups.

Wrap-Up

It is fun to think about what you have in common with your character. It is interesting that some of you, even though your character is an animal, could find things that are the same! Many people have similar traits, but also have things that make them different. That is what makes each one of us so special.

DAY 14 Guided Practice

Focused Instruction

Yesterday we thought about ourselves in relation to our characters. Today we are going to think about everything we have learned over the last few weeks about our characters and write it on the character web. Think back to all of the things you have noticed as you took time to read the books from your series.

- Model completing part of character web on Olivia.

Independent Practice

- Distribute Character Web (Resource 3.9).

Your reading work today is to list with your groups everything you can think of to fill in your web about your character. Name all of the traits that make your character special, both physical and personality traits.

Wrap-Up

Today we named lots of things about our characters. Turn to the group next to you and share some of the things you learned about your character over the last few weeks.

DAY 15 Commitment

Focused Instruction

We have spent the last three weeks deeply studying a character in a series book. Today we are going to reflect on our learning to prepare us for our Character Club writing unit. Let's think about Olivia. If we were going to write another book to add to the Olivia series, what would be some of the most important things about her character that would influence the story in this new book?

- Chart responses about Olivia. Many of the responses will be things you have already talked about, but this is to help prepare for the writing unit to follow.

Independent Practice

- Distribute What We Have Learned (Resource 3.10).

Your reading work today is to think about your character and record as much as you can about his or her physical and personality traits. You may even be able to think about a title for a new series based on all of the things you learned about your character.

Wrap-Up

We have spent the last three weeks studying our characters, and now you are all experts on your characters. Now when you read books in a series, you will have a sense of how the characters guide us through the story.

The World of Characters

Your students have been building their stamina, readying themselves for this longer unit on character. This strategy unit is intensely connected to the reading unit in character, and at this point your students should be fully prepared for the excitement of creating their own series books. They know and love their characters and are ready to fall inside those worlds and become part of them.

Writing a New Series Book: Character Clubs

STRATEGY

Why Teach This?

- To help students see the connection between reading and writing.
- To show students that they can use what they know about characters to create their own stories.
- To validate that students are authors just like the authors of series books they love.

Framing Questions

- How do we take what we know about a character and transform it into a series book?
- How do we work with a collaborative group to create a book?

Unit Goals

- Students will use what they know about a character to create a book.
- Students will use planning sheets to support their writing.
- Students will show evidence of how a series works in their own writing.
- Students will work collaboratively to create a series book.

Anchor Texts

- Dragon books by Dav Pilkey
- Fluffy books by Kate McMullan
- Henry and Mudge books by Cynthia Rylant
- Olivia books by Ian Falconer
- Poppleton books by Cynthia Rylant

Resource Sheets

- Possible Titles (Resource 3.11)
- Editing Checklist (Resource 3.12)

Unit Assessment Writing a New Series Book: Character Clubs			STRATEGY
Student name:	EMERGING	DEVELOPING	INDEPENDENT
Works collaboratively on a piece of writing.			
Shows evidence of character traits in a piece of writing.			
Understands how to use plan sheets to support extended writing.			
Shows knowledge of story elements by replicating them in his or her own writing.			

Stage of the Unit	Focused Instruction You will	Independent Practice Students will
IMMERSION 1 day	• discuss how we will write our own version of a character series using what we know about our characters. • study Olivia as a character and model discussion through whole-class character study. • write some possible titles for a whole-class book.	• meet with character clubs and discuss possible ideas for their own books to add to the character series.
IDENTIFICATION 1 day	• name ideas for a whole-class book using one of the series' characters they know, such as Olivia.	• meet with their character clubs to discuss and chart big ideas for their own stories.
GUIDED PRACTICE 7 days	• model the procedures for creating a "kickoff" or beginning that gets the reader's attention in your new series book. • model the procedures for working on the events that will comprise the middle of the book, making sure the events happen in order. • model the procedures for rereading the story before adding to it. • create a "tie-up" or ending for the book that makes it sound like the book is over. • model the procedures for rereading and revising content in your new series book. • model the procedures for rereading and editing your new series book, checking conventions of writing.	• meet with character clubs to work on creating their series books, working together to do the following: • creating a kickoff or beginning that gets the reader's attention • working on the events in the middle of the book, making sure the events happen in order • creating a tie-up or ending for the book that makes it sound like the book is finished • rereading and revising content • rereading and editing, checking conventions of writing • publishing the book, adding a cover and title

COMMITMENT 1 day	• reflect on how studying a series can allow us to transfer our knowledge into the writing of a series book.	• celebrate their hard work and share their addition to the series with other groups in the class.
TOTAL: 10 DAYS		

EARLY FALL

LATE FALL

WINTER

SPRING

Getting Started

In order to be successful in this unit, children will have to look back at their plan sheets from the Investigating Characters: Character Clubs unit which will help support their thinking about their character. They will begin to formulate ideas about how to write their stories.

Structures and Routines

The structures and routines for this unit remain the same as they have been for writing time throughout the school year. Students will work during writing time with their groups to create the new book for the series they've been studying.

Teaching Materials

Since this strategy unit relies heavily on the reading unit you have just completed, students will need few materials except for the work from the Character Clubs reading unit and some anchor texts.

Dear Parents,

We have just finished studying characters in a book series we read in class. Now we are going to use what we know to write our own book for the series. We will work in our character clubs to think about the characters and write a new story together. The goals of this unit include:

- using what we have learned about a series to create our own book for the series
- taking character traits we have learned about to help us write a new adventure for the character
- working with a group to create a story
- thinking about our knowledge of story elements to help support our writing
- using plan sheets as a tool to create writing

To continue to support this work at home, please have conversations about characters in books. The more we understand a character in a book, the better our comprehension is of the story.

Warmly,

Above is a letter you can send to parents to help support their children's learning in this unit.

Differentiation

Within this unit, students will work at their own pace. As the teacher, you will confer with students individually, supporting them based on need and helping them to contribute to the group project.

Stages of the Unit

Immersion

During the reading unit, students were immersed in their specific series books and spent time getting to know the characters. They are now prepared to move on to the writing phase. At the beginning of this unit, send a letter home to parents to encourage them to support this work.

Identification

Help students plan the big idea for their book. They will think about what the main idea will be and what will happen in the book, including the beginning, middle, and ending. Students will do this work through conversation and record their ideas on the book planning page. This page will help them as they move into Guided Practice and begin writing their books.

Guided Practice

Students work on writing their book as a team. The lessons during this time will help support the group as writers by focusing on how to write a strong beginning, a middle with detailed information, and an ending that makes the book sound like it is finished.

Commitment

Now is the time to edit, publish, and share these stories. Have your children reflect on how this unit went for them and how their book shows strong evidence of their knowledge of the character studied. Here is an example of a chart we built with our class which summed up some of their learning:

Name of Character Club	Main Idea of Series Book Created	Shows understanding of
Poppleton	*Poppleton Goes to School* Poppleton has a hard time in math and Cherry Sue helps him learn so he does better in school.	• the importance of Poppleton's friendships and how they support him through challenges. • structure of the Poppleton series: problem followed by a solution.
Toad	*Where's Toad?* When Frog goes to find Toad, he finds Toad lost under his clothes. Frog helps Toad clean up and organize his house.	• Frog as a character: Frog is always responsible. • character relationships: Toad needs Frog to help him through life's challenges. • Toad as a character: Toad is messy.

Assessment

The assessment for this unit will be ongoing. Your job is to note the following during conferences:

- How are my students working together as a group?
- Did my students create a book that shows evidence of series and character knowledge?
- Do my students use planning sheets to help them support their writing?
- Do my students have knowledge of story elements and how stories work when writing them?

The goal of this unit, to have students write a series book to add to a series they have been studying, will also reveal what they learned during the previous reading unit. You will be able to assess whether the students are transferring their knowledge from the fall unit of narrative reading and writing.

Day-by-Day Lessons

DAY 1 Immersion

Focused Instruction

We've spent the last few weeks getting to know characters and their behaviors in our character clubs. Now we are going to write our own group book to add to the series we have been reading. This book will be a new adventure for the character in which something new happens to him or her.

*But first, as a whole class, we are going to write a group book about another adventure that Olivia goes on. Let's take a minute to think about a title for a new Olivia book. Remember the books we have read and studied—*Olivia, Olivia Saves the Circus, Olivia and the Missing Toy, *and* Olivia Forms a Band? *In all of these books, Olivia has a lot of energy and a great imagination. Let's think of another adventure Olivia could have. Turn and talk to the person next to you and think of some titles for our new book.*

- Students turn and talk about possible titles and adventures.
- Chart the titles that pairs come up with.
- Vote on a class title for the new Olivia book.

Independent Practice

- Distribute the Possible Titles Sheet (Resource 3.11).

Your writing work today is to meet with your character club and talk about some ideas you have for the next adventure of your character. Use the What We Have Learned plan sheet from Day 15 of our reading unit to help you think about the character and some possible ideas for the book. We are trying to think of a new adventure for the character. You can think of a few titles like we did for the Olivia books and then work as a club to pick one that you want to start writing tomorrow. Use the top of your Possible Titles sheet to name the titles and then circle the one you vote on as a group. Remember to fill out only the top of this sheet today.

- Students work with their clubs to think of a title for the book they will be writing.

Wrap-Up

Today each character club thought of a title for the book they will be writing over the next two weeks. Let's share our titles with the other character clubs.

DAY 2 Identification

Focused Instruction

We are ready to begin to think about the big idea in our book—what is going to happen to the character during the adventure. Let's try this with Olivia. Yesterday we decided that our book is going to be called Olivia Goes to the Park. *Let's think about the big idea, what will happen to Olivia in this book. We will think about the kickoff event, three events that will follow, and the tie-up.*

- Students turn and talk about what they think would be a good story about Olivia in the park.
- Have students chart their ideas.

Title of Book	Kickoff	Event
Olivia Goes to the Park	Olivia goes to the park and there are a lot of other young pigs there.	Olivia pretends she is being chased by a big monster (really it is just another pig).
Event	**Event**	**Tie-up**
Olivia hides inside the big pipe that is used as a tunnel.	Olivia runs as fast as she can and shoots up on the swings like a rocket.	Olivia's mom decides that she is being too silly and that she should just play with her little brother at the park instead.

Independent Practice

Your writing work today is to meet with your club and work on the big ideas for your book. Remember to think of a kickoff, three events, and the tie-up. Use your sheet from yesterday to record your thinking.

- Students discuss in their clubs what they want to happen in their book.

Wrap-Up

Today we thought of the big ideas for our books. This planning will help us with our writing work tomorrow. Turn to the club next to you and tell them what happens in your book.

DAY 3 Guided Practice

Focused Instruction

We now have a plan for our series book. Today we are going to work on our beginnings, using our plan to help us. A good beginning or kickoff event gets the reader's attention and makes him want to read the rest of the book. Some of the ways to get the reader's attention are:

- *asking a question*
- *using words that make a picture in your mind*
- *posing a problem*
- *using ellipses to show more is coming*

You can look at how some of the books in your series have strong beginnings that get the reader's attention. Let's write the beginning for the Olivia book. Remember yesterday we said that in the beginning Olivia goes to the park and there are a lot of other young pigs there. Let's try to add some more words to this and write them on the page.

Independent Practice

Your writing work is to look back at your plan sheet and use your notes to write the kickoff to your book. Remember to add to the words you already have and put it on writing paper. Make sure to make a picture to match your words.

- Students work on the kickoff event for their books.

Wrap-Up

We all wrote really strong kickoff events today. Tomorrow we will begin to work on the middle of the book, the events that will happen in the story.

DAY 4 Guided Practice

Focused Instruction

To begin to work on the events in our book, take out your plan sheets. As we planned our new book about Olivia, we talked about some events that happened to her in the park. Let's write this page of our story together to see what we can add on to the event to tell more about it.

- Students work with you on the rug to draft the next page in the book using the first event from the plan sheet as a guideline.
- Write the words for this part of the book up on chart paper, modeling writing for your students.

Independent Practice

Your writing work today and for the next few days is to work with your club on creating the middle of your book, when the events take place. Remember to use your plan sheet to help you. The plan sheet has the events in order. Your job is to add to the events and make pictures to match your words.

- Students work on writing the next page of their book, the first event in the story.

Wrap-Up

Turn to the club next to you and share the event you wrote today. Read it to them and have the group think about whether your event makes sense.

DAY 5 Guided Practice

Focused Instruction

The middle of the book is the meat of the story. It is the part where we have to fill in the events that happen to the character and what the character does. To make sure the middle of the story makes sense, we need to reread our writing from yesterday and then add to it. Let's add an event to the class Olivia book first.

Independent Practice

Continue to work with your club to add events to the middle of your series book.

Wrap-Up

Turn and share your middle events with another character club.

DAY 6 Guided Practice

Focused Instruction

We are going to continue to add one more event to our Olivia book.

Independent Practice

Continue to work on adding events to your group series book.

Wrap-Up

Share the middle of your book with another group.

DAY 7 Guided Practice

Focused Instruction

We have spent the last few days working on the events in our book. Today we are going to work on the tie-up or the ending. Remember, the tie-up makes it sound like the story is over. It is also the place where any problems or actions in the story come to an end or a close. Before we write an ending, we need to reread what we already have in our books. Let's reread what we have written for our Olivia book and then use our plan sheet to help us write the ending. What would make the Olivia book come to an end and sound like it is over?

- Reread the writing of the Olivia book so far.
- Have students discuss some possible ways to write the ending.
- Write the ending on chart paper, modeling writing strategies for the class.

Independent Practice

Your writing work is to write the ending to your book. The first thing you need to do with your group is reread what you have already written so that the ending can flow from your writing. Remember to check your plan sheet to see what you have written for the tie-up.

- Students work on writing the tie-up of their books.

Wrap-Up

Today we wrote the endings to our stories. You have all done a wonderful job working together with your club and writing a new book to add to your series. By the end of this week we will celebrate the hard work we have done!

DAY 8 Guided Practice

Focused Instruction

One thing that writers do is revise and edit their work. To revise our work we look at the words, the actual writing, and see if there are any ways to make it better. We may add more to our words. We may take something away that does not make sense. Today we are going to revise our stories. Let's listen to our Olivia book and see if there are any places to add to the words, make something more clear for the reader, or make the writing sound better.

- Create a chart like the one below and share with students.

> Writers revise their work. Revising means making the actual writing better.
> Some ways to try this:
> - add more to your words
> - add descriptive language
> - reread and rewrite the way you said something so it makes more sense
> - try to say something in a different way

- Read the class version of *Olivia Goes to the Park*.
- Take suggestions for places to add to the work or make it better. If there are no suggestions, model some ways to add to the writing or make it better.

Independent Practice

Your writing work is to reread and find some places to revise. You need to find at least one place with your group to make your writing better.

- Students work on rereading their series book and revising.

Wrap-Up

All of you found a place to revise your writing. Let's share these revisions with another club.

DAY 9 Guided Practice

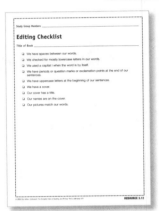

Focused Instruction

- Distribute the Editing Checklist (Resource 3.12).

Yesterday we revised our writing by adding on and making our work stronger and better. Today we are going to do some editing using an editing checklist. When we edit we are looking at spacing of words, punctuation, and spelling. When we edit we are making our writing ready for others to read it. First we need to check for the things listed on the Editing Checklist, and then we can check off these items on the list.

Independent Practice

Your writing work is to read through your books and edit, using the editing checklist as your guideline. When you finish editing, you can work on making a cover for your books.

- Students read through the books and edit.
- Students work on the cover for their books.

Wrap-Up

All of you made amazing stories to add to the series collection. Tomorrow we are going to celebrate our writing, share our stories, and put our stories in the library in the basket with the other books in the series!

DAY 10 Commitment

Focused Instruction

All of you have written terrific stories using what you know about your characters and about the series you studied. Today we are going to have a writing celebration. We are going to share our stories with our classmates.

- Break students up into groups of two character clubs each and have them share their stories.
- Give students small pieces of paper to write down compliments of the other groups' writing. Each person in the group should write a compliment to another member of the group.

Independent Practice

Your writing work is to listen to your friends read their stories. While they are reading, you need to listen, and when they are finished write them a complimentary note about their book. You can tell them if there is a funny part, or something you liked about the character, or anything else you can think of to tell the group that is positive.

Wrap-Up

All of you did a wonderful job listening to and complimenting each other. Now we will put our stories into the series baskets and you can read them during Independent Practice.

From Late Fall to Winter

Your first graders have been immersed in the world of story. As winter arrives and your students become even more familiar with the books in your classroom, they are increasing their literacy skills as they talk with partners and investigate characters. Now they are ready to enter the world of nonfiction—navigating a genre they love to read with more confidence than ever before.

Chapter 4

WINTER

The First Grader as Explorer of Language and Ideas

"Different kinds of flowers have different shapes and numbers of petals. But all flowers make seeds that will grow into new plants."
—from *Flowers, Fruits, and Seeds* by Angela Royston

Your first graders are blossoming. During this season, they navigate through nonfiction texts and learn to revise with greater confidence. They are exploring the beauty and mysteries of language through units designed to support their inquiries into print. Come with us as we explore units that match the journeys of our young explorers.

WINTER UNITS

- Navigating Nonfiction, *page 102*
- Creating All-About Books: Nonfiction, *page 117*
- Developing Print Strategies: Readers Reread and Revise, *page 131*
- Enhancing Our Writing: Revision Strategies, *page 134*
- Making Meaning: Connecting Across Genres, *page 136*

SPOTLIGHT UNITS

SPOTLIGHT on Genre

- Navigating Nonfiction
- Creating All-About Books: Nonfiction

There are a few great writers who have been able to write across several genres. E. B. White comes to mind. He wrote the classic children's books *Charlotte's Web*, *The Trumpet of the Swan*, and *Stuart Little*. He wrote small humorous snippets for *The New Yorker* in the Talk of the Town column. And, he cowrote the seminal "how-to" guide to grammar: *The Elements of Style*. White was the rare genius who could accommodate all genres, fitting his observations, his wonderings, his memory, and his imagination into a wide variety of "containers."

Great ideas are like water, flowing clear: a stream. Genre is a container we use to hold those ideas. The ideas are the same, but they look different depending on the container that holds them. Loneliness inside a poem, for example, looks different from loneliness inside a science fiction novel. Courage inside a biography looks different from courage inside a letter. A clear idea, held inside the right container can change someone's mind, even someone's life. See pages 47–61 in my book *The Complete 4 for Literacy* for a more detailed description of the elements and categories of genre and the importance of these units to the lives of our students. They are seeking to clarify, extend, and share from their own stream of ideas.

Pam Allyn

First Graders Love the World of Facts

First graders are joyously curious, buoyantly open, and endlessly questioning. They can barely go to sleep at night for all the questions swimming inside their ever-active heads. We are constantly trying to figure out how to respond to their questions, which are generally a combination of fact-seeking missiles and existential philosophical mediations on the nature of the universe. Units in nonfiction provide them with ways to learn about how this genre functions and how they can use it to answer some of the questions they hunger to know more about. As first graders, they feel big in the world now, and so the All-About Books writing unit is an excellent companion. The world is expansive and so are they—exploring topics of interest to them and sharing all about it with friends and family. Research has shown that 86 percent of the texts read by adults are nonfiction, and yet only 30 to 40 percent of the texts students are exposed to are nonfiction. In *Nonfiction in Focus*, Kristo and Bamford (2004) note that "perhaps the most compelling reason for the rising tide of nonfiction is the possible impact it has on students. When you incorporate high-quality nonfiction into your program, you help students in many ways. Specifically you

- meet the needs of students with a range of reading levels and interests.
- provide examples of writing in various content areas.
- open the door to classroom research and inquiry.
- develop and expand vocabulary.
- influence growth and development of primary-grade readers and writers."

The icing on this cake is that your students will love studying nonfiction! Their curious minds are seeking and seeking, and their bountiful hearts are giving and giving. These units are a perfect match for those inclinations.

Navigating Nonfiction   GENRE

Why Teach This?
- To expose children to nonfiction and help them navigate nonfiction text.
- To show children how fiction and nonfiction are different.
- To expose children to different nonfiction structures.
- To show children the many ways we can get information from nonfiction text.

Framing Questions
- What is the difference between a fiction and nonfiction text?
- What strategies and skills do we need to read nonfiction books?
- What are the different nonfiction structures?

Unit Goals
- Students will understand the differences between fiction and nonfiction.
- Students will be exposed to different nonfiction structures: all-about books, how-to books, narrative nonfiction, reference books, and question-and-answer books.

- Students will be familiar with and be able to identify the following features: table of contents, layout, headings, labels, captions, glossary, index, diagrams, photographs, and print type.
- Students will work in a collaborative group to study nonfiction books.

Anchor Texts

- *A Field Full of Horses* by Peter Hansard
- *Meet the Octopus* by Sylvia James
- *Polar Lands* by Margaret Hynes
- *The Supermarket* by Kathleen Krull
- *Surprising Sharks* by Nicola Davies
- *What Do You Do With a Tail Like This?* by Robin Page and Steve Jenkins

Resource Sheets

- Nonfiction Features Chart One (Resource 4.1)
- Nonfiction Features Chart Two (Resource 4.2)
- Questions About Our Topic (Resource 4.3)
- Picture Search (Resource 4.4)
- Nonfiction Fact Sheet (Resource 4.5)
- Nonfiction Homework (Resource 4.6)
- Nonfiction Feature Detectives (Resource 4.7)
- Feature Detectives Comparison (Resource 4.8)
- Vocabulary Detectives (Resource 4.9)
- Nonfiction Vocabulary Homework (Resource 4.10)
- Nonfiction Project Plan (Resource 4.11)

Unit Assessment Navigating Nonfiction			GENRE
Student name:	EMERGING	DEVELOPING	INDEPENDENT
Works collaboratively studying a topic.			
Understands the difference between fact and opinion.			
Poses questions about a topic and looks for the answer within a nonfiction book.			
Identifies differences between nonfiction structures.			
Names and identifies specific nonfiction features.			
Uses nonfiction features to navigate nonfiction text.			

Stage of the Unit	Focused Instruction You will	Independent Practice Students will
IMMERSION 3 days	• discuss differences between fiction and nonfiction books; sort favorite read-alouds into two piles: fiction and nonfiction. • create a "What Do We Already Know About Nonfiction?" chart. • name the features in a nonfiction text.	• explore the differences between fiction and nonfiction books. • put sticky notes on observations in a nonfiction book. • put sticky notes on features they notice in a nonfiction book.
IDENTIFICATION 3 days	• name and identify nonfiction structures in reference books. • read aloud from *What Do You Do With a Tail Like This?* to name and identify nonfiction structures in question-and-answer books. • read aloud from *Growing Radishes and Carrots* and name and identify nonfiction structures in how-to books.	• browse nonfiction books looking specifically at nonfiction structures; identify and name features. • choose a nonfiction study topic. • determine how features and structures help us navigate through nonfiction.
GUIDED PRACTICE 6 days	• pick one whole-class study to support this work based on the books you have; think of two questions about your topic. • study a picture in *Meet the Octopus* and record four observations. • research an answer to the two questions about your topic; discuss the difference between fact and opinion. • use *Meet the Octopus* to look for nonfiction features; name the features of nonfiction text. • compare features across two nonfiction texts, such as *The Supermarket* and *Surprising Sharks*. • find new vocabulary words related to topic and define them.	• work in nonfiction study groups and think of two questions to answer during the study; complete a plan sheet. • study a picture and record their observations; complete the Picture Search Sheet. • work in nonfiction study groups and answer their two questions. • use the Features Detective Checklist to record features they find in their books. • compare the features across various nonfiction texts. • find new vocabulary words related to their topic and define them.
COMMITMENT 4 days	• reflect on learning about whole-class topic and create a class mural showing learning (see photos later in the chapter).	• commit to their topic and create a poster showing what their study group has learned. • celebrate and share group posters (see photos later in the chapter).
TOTAL: 16 DAYS		

Getting Started

This unit works smoothly when it follows the unit on character clubs, since students continue to work collaboratively in small groups. In this unit students will choose a topic by interest and work in small reading clubs to study the topic together.

Structures and Routines

Students now understand the routines of working in a group and having conversations with others around a topic. Throughout the unit, the class will be studying a nonfiction topic to continuously model the work happening in the small groups. This topic can be selected by you or your students and should be based on interest and resources.

After each day's Independent Practice (primarily based in study-group work), the class will gather again to share, looking closely at what children have done in their study group for the day.

Teaching Materials

Each group will need a pocket folder to hold their work for these three weeks. In addition, each student should have a basket or plastic bag filled with books on a specific topic. Books can be of varying levels since much of the work will require navigating through features and using the photographs, not just the text. The categories for the nonfiction topics can be based on the kinds of nonfiction books in the classroom and/or the resources available at the local or school library.

There are many new and exciting nonfiction books available for children and many publishing companies are now focusing on creating leveled nonfiction books for children. Following are a variety of resources to support this unit.

Nonfiction Series

- About series (Peachtree Publishers)
- Discoveries series (Barnes & Noble Publishing)
- DK Eyewitness Books (DK Children)
- Eye-Openers (Simon & Schuster)
- First Discovery (Scholastic)
- I Wonder Why (Scholastic)
- Read and Wonder (Candlewick Press)
- Rookie Readers (Scholastic)
- Science Vocabulary Readers (Scholastic)
- Time for Kids (Time Magazine)

Read-Alouds Categorized by Structure

EARLY FALL

LATE FALL

WINTER

SPRING

Informational Picture Books or Narrative	All-About Books	Reference Books	Question-and-Answer Books	How-To Books
Chameleons are Cool by Martin Jenkins	*Sharks* by Janet Palazzo Craig	*Scholastic Atlas of Earth*	*What's Inside?* by Mary J. Martin	*Growing Radishes and Carrots* by Faye Bolton and Diane Snowball
Tony the Tokay Gecko by John Storms	*Robots* by Clive Gifford	*The Usborne First Encyclopedia Series*	*Do Cowboys Ride Bikes?* by Kathy Tucker	*Growing Frogs* by Vivian French
A Field Full of Horses by Peter Hansard	*Hygiene and Health* by Claire Llewellyn	*Beginners World Atlas* (National Geographic)	*Tails* by Marcia Vaughan	*How to Make Salsa* by Jamie Lucero
All Pigs are Beautiful by Dick King-Smith	*I Love Guinea Pigs* by Dick King-Smith	*The World Almanac For Kids*	*I Wonder Why Snakes Shed Their Skin and Other Questions About Reptiles* by Amanda O'Neill	*Mom and Me Cookbook* by Annabel Karmel
T-Rex by Vivian French	*My Visit to the Aquarium* by Aliki		*Flowers, Fruits, and Seeds* by Angela Royston	*How to Draw Insects* by Christine Smith
	Seashore by Steve Parker		*What Do You Do With a Tail Like This?* by Robin Page and Steve Jenkins	
			Do Animals Take Baths? by Neil Morris and Toni Goffe	
			Why Do Cats Purr? by Apple Jordan	

Publishers of Nonfiction Series and Texts

- National Geographic for Kids (www.ngschoolpuborg)
- Mondo Publishing (www.mondopub.com)
- Scholastic (www.scholastic.com)
- Newbridge (www.newbridgeonline.com)

Stages of the Unit

Immersion

Spend some time differentiating and sorting fiction from nonfiction with your students. Focus on noticing features and navigating text in nonfiction books. A letter to the parents will go home at the beginning of this unit to encourage families to support your work.

Identification

Introduce the names of different nonfiction structures, including narrative books or informational picture books (books that sound like stories but give nonfiction information), reference books, question-and-answer books, how-to books, and all-about books.

Guided Practice

Children will begin to navigate nonfiction text modeled through whole-group instruction and practiced in their study groups. Focus on using pictures to get information, naming and noticing features and how they help us to navigate through nonfiction text, and learning new information about a topic. This work will take place in the whole group, with a class nonfiction topic, and in small groups, with children studying the topics of their choice.

Commitment

Students will create a collage poster with their group, showing facts and information about their nonfiction study topics. Students will reflect on the week's work, looking back at plan sheets to create the project together.

> Dear Parents,
>
> We are beginning our nonfiction unit in reading, which will be followed by our nonfiction unit in writing. The purpose of these units is to expose your children to the exciting genre of nonfiction. The content of the reading unit includes:
>
> - thinking about how to read nonfiction and how that is different from reading fiction
> - learning how to navigate through nonfiction text using the features
> - finding facts
> - using the photographs to get information
> - using this new knowledge about nonfiction to then create our own nonfiction writing piece
>
> In order to support our work, feel free to check out lots of nonfiction books from the library and spend time scanning and sifting though nonfiction texts with your child.
>
> Warmly,

Above is a letter you can send to parents to help support their children's learning in this unit.

Assessment

The assessment for this unit will take place while conferring with groups and taking notes during whole-class instruction. Here are guiding questions for conferences in this unit:

- How is nonfiction different from fiction?
- What kinds of features are in this book, and how do they help you as a reader?
- What can you learn from looking at the pictures in this book?
- What are the facts, and are there any opinions in this text?
- How can you navigate through this text? How do you know what to read first?
- What are the similarities and differences across some of these nonfiction books?

Day-by-Day Lessons

DAY 1 Immersion

Focused Instruction

Readers read many different kinds of books. Throughout this school year we have read both fiction and nonfiction books. Today we are going to use what we know to sort some of our favorite read-alouds into two piles: one fiction pile and one nonfiction pile. Remember, a fiction book is one that is not true, and a nonfiction book is one that gives us true information.

Independent Practice

Your reading work today is to work with your partner to sort the books I have given you into fiction and nonfiction piles. Remember to think about why you sorted each book the way you did.

- Students sort books into fiction and nonfiction piles with their partners.

Wrap-Up

Today we made fiction and nonfiction piles. Turn to the pair next to you and show them one fiction book and one nonfiction book. Discuss how you decided which pile the books went into. Let's also write the titles in the read-aloud sort.

Read-Aloud Sort	
Fiction	**Nonfiction**
Smiley Shark	Surprising Sharks
Owen	What's Inside?

DAY 2 Immersion

Focused Instruction

Please take out your baskets of nonfiction books. What do we know about the pictures, the print type, or other features that are different from fiction books?

- Chart students' answers to the question "What do we already know about nonfiction?"

Independent Practice

Your reading work today is to look through the nonfiction baskets on your tables. Use sticky notes to post things you notice in nonfiction books.

- Students use sticky notes to post observations in nonfiction books.

Wrap-Up

We all posted observations today in our nonfiction books. What are some things that you noticed?

DAY 3 Immersion

Focused Instruction

For the past two days we have been looking at many different nonfiction books. Nonfiction books have features. The features give us information in different ways. Here is a chart of some of the features we can find in nonfiction books.

- Include a picture of each feature. You can copy one from a book to put up on the poster.

These charts can be used for the whole class or to give out to partnerships.

Independent Practice

Your reading work today is to look for books with a table of contents, headings, and captions. When you find one of these features, put a sticky note on that page. Talk about what information these features give you as you read. We will then put these sticky notes on the features chart to see what features we have found.

- Students browse books and notice features.

Wrap-Up

We all found some features today. Let's put our sticky notes on the features chart.

DAY 4 Identification

Focused Instruction

We have been immersing ourselves in informational picture book and "all-about" nonfiction texts. Another kind of nonfiction book is a reference book. Reference books are often long books with a lot of information and can be the hardest to look at because there is so much to see. You may find some new features in these books.

- Here is a chart to support the work for the next three days, adding one or two types of book definition each day:

Structures or Types of Nonfiction

REFERENCE BOOKS
- Give information in a different format (like in dictionaries, encyclopedias, atlases, etc.).

INFORMATIONAL PICTURE BOOKS (Narrative)
- Narrative nonfiction sounds like a story but has factual information. It often also has opinions.

ALL-ABOUT BOOKS
- All-about books give a lot of information about a topic.

QUESTION-AND-ANSWER BOOKS
- Question-and-answer books have a question-and-answer format.

HOW-TO BOOKS
- How-to books tell the reader how to do something, like a cookbook or a do-it-yourself book.

Types of Nonfiction

Informational Picture Storybooks
- sounds like a story but has factual information

All About Books
- gives a lot of information about a topic

Reference Books
- has a lot of facts like in a dictionary encyclopedia or an atlas

Question and Answer Books
- books that have a question and an answer

How-to Books
- tells you how to do things (recipes, art projects...)

You can create a chart naming different kinds of nonfiction books and their features.

Independent Practice

Your reading work today is to look at a reference book with your partner. Try to see if you can find some new features, different from the ones you have found so far. You may be able to find a map or a map key in these kinds of books. Post the features you find so we can add them to our features chart.

- Students look through reference books.

Wrap-Up

Today we looked at reference books and posted features. Let's record some of the work we have found on our features chart. What kinds of features did you find and what did you learn from the features?

Nonfiction Features		
Name it	Where I found it	What does it tell us?
label	next to a picture of a spider	the part of the spider's middle is called the "abdomen"
heading		
diagram		

- This chart can be ongoing throughout the reading unit; students can add to it as they work in independent reading or with partners.

DAY 5 Identification

Focused Instruction

A question-and-answer book always has a question followed by an answer on the same page or on different pages. Question-and-answer books may also fall under the all-about book category. Let's look at this question-and-answer book together. It is called What's Inside? by Mary J. Martin. Each page has a question followed by an answer to the question on the next page.

Independent Practice

Your reading work is to continue to look for nonfiction features in nonfiction books. If you find any of the kinds of books we have talked about, make sure to put a sticky note on the front of the book labeling the kind of book it is. If you find an informational picture book put an IP, if you find a reference book put an R, and so on.

- Students look at a few different kinds of nonfiction books with partners and discuss the structure of the book.

Wrap-Up

Share your sticky notes. What features did you find in the nonfiction books?

DAY 6 Identification

Focused Instruction

A how-to book tells you how to do something. Some examples of how-to books are recipe books, books about taking care of a garden or a pet, books that tell you how to do an art project, and many others. Let's look at this how-to book together. It is called Growing Radishes and Carrots. *As you read various how-to books, begin to think about what topic you'd like to study.*

- Browse *Growing Radishes and Carrots* as a class.

Independent Practice

Your reading work today is to see if you can find any how-to books. After you find some, spend time thinking about what topic you want to learn more about. Pick three and fill out a topic choice sheet (see example). *I will make sure you get one of your choices.*

Wrap-Up

Today we looked at how-to books. What are some of the things that your books told you how to do?

- At the end of this day, students will have signed up for a nonfiction study topic. The topics for the groups should be based on books available in the classroom or books accessible in the library. After children choose their top three choices, form heterogeneous groups of students who work well together. Below is an example of study groups:

Nonfiction Study Groups		
Ocean Animals Yi Jake Shinchul Claire	**Food and Recipes** Thomas Patrick Jamal Christine	**Land Animals** Malik Elizabeth Amy Jordi
Space Chayim Alec Hannah Natalia	**Insects and Bugs** Julian Greg Mriganka Sidrat	

(Study groups for this unit should include no more than four students, so you may have six or seven groups depending on your class size.)

DAY 7 Guided Practice

Focused Instruction

- Distribute Questions About Our Topic (Resource 4.3).

We have studied different kinds of nonfiction structures and will now focus on one nonfiction topic together as a class. Our class topic is going to be octopus. Please think about two questions we might want to research during our study.

The class topic can be anything that students will want to know more about. It also can be based on what books are available to support the work.

Independent Practice

Your reading work today is to meet with your study group and think of two questions you want to find the answers to during your study. Record the questions on the plan sheet. When you finish, put the plan sheet in your new nonfiction group folder. Then take some time to decorate the folder with pictures that match your topic and remember to include your names.

Wrap-Up

Today we made our topic folders. Share your folder with another group.

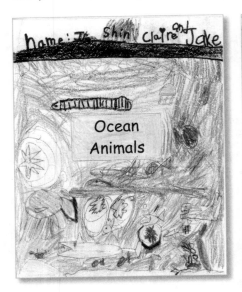

DAY 8 Guided Practice

Focused Instruction

Sometimes when we look at nonfiction books, there are a lot of tricky parts that are hard to read. Good readers also look at the pictures to find information. Let's choose one picture and list four things we can learn just from studying it.

- Model how to get information from pictures about the whole-class topic, using a Big Book or read-aloud. Look closely at a picture and list four things the children learn from looking at the picture. Choose one picture only.

Independent Practice

- Distribute Picture Search (Resource 4.4).

Your reading work today is to meet with your group and look at a picture from one of your books. Choose one picture with a lot of details. Then write down on your Picture Search four things you notice from looking at the picture.

Wrap-Up

Turn to the group next to you. Show them the picture your group chose and share one thing that you learned from looking at the picture.

DAY 9 Guided Practice

Focused Instruction

Remember our questions from two days ago? Let's look in this Big Book about octopuses to see if we can answer our questions. We may find some other facts. A fact is something we can prove is true. Sometimes, we can confuse a fact with an opinion, which is something we think or feel.

- You may wish to create a chart like the one below to share with students.

Fact versus Opinion
A fact is something we can prove is true. (The sky is blue.)
An opinion is something we think or feel. (I love guinea pigs.)

Independent Practice

- Distribute Nonfiction Fact Sheet (Resource 4.5).

Work with your study group to look through the books about your topic and see if you can find the answers to the questions you wrote a few days ago. You may find new information or facts (something we can prove is true) as you are researching. If you cannot find the answers, that is okay. We can also look in other resources on another day. When you finish, record the new facts you found on the fact plan sheet.

Wrap-Up

Some of us found the answers to some of our questions today. Some of us did not find the answers. Books are one place we can get information. Other places we can look for answers are on the Internet or we can ask an expert. Over the next few days you may want to see if you can find the answers to your questions somewhere else.

- Send home the Nonfiction Homework (Resource 4.6).

DAY 10 Guided Practice

Focused Instruction

So far we have found a lot of new information about octopuses by looking at the pictures and researching our questions. Another way to find information is to look at the features. As we have learned, different nonfiction books have different features. Today we are going to be feature detectives. A detective is someone who searches and finds something. We are going to search for features in our Meet the Octopus Big Book.

- Model searching for features using the Big Book.

Independent Practice

- Distribute Nonfiction Features Detectives (Resource 4.7).

Each one of you is to pick one book from your study group basket or plastic bag. Use the Feature Detective checklist to record which features you find in your book.

- Students will work on finding features in the book they choose.

Wrap-Up

You were all very good detectives today and found many different features in your books. Tomorrow we are going to compare our books to see what features are in most of the books.

DAY 11 Guided Practice

Focused Instruction

Features give us information in a text. We are learning that not all features appear in all books. Look at these two octopus books.

- Show an all-about book and an informational picture book.

One of these books has a table of contents and one does not. One has a glossary and the other does not. Both books have captions and labels.

Independent Practice

- Distribute the Feature Detectives Comparison sheet (Resource 4.8).

Your reading work today is to look at your Feature Detective sheets with your group. Use the Feature Comparison sheet to look across the books and compare which books on your topics have the same features and which books have different features.

Wrap-Up

We compared the features we found in different books today. What were the features that were in most of the books?

- Chart the most common features as a class.

DAY 12 Guided Practice

Focused Instruction

We have spent the last few days learning all about octopuses while each of you is learning about your own nonfiction topics. When we read, skim, and scan nonfiction books, we learn a lot of new information. We also came across a lot of new words, vocabulary words like funnel, ink, *and* octopus.

Independent Practice

- Distribute Vocabulary Detectives (Resource 4.9).

Your reading work today is to record some new vocabulary words using the Vocabulary Detectives sheet. You will find a lot of new words related to your topic. When you come across an unknown word, use the other words around it and the pictures to help you think about what it may mean.

- Students work together to look in a book from their nonfiction study basket searching for new vocabulary words (in glossaries, too).
- Send home the Nonfiction Vocabulary Homework (Resource 4.10).

Wrap-Up

We all learned many new vocabulary words today. Now we are going to list some of them and discuss their meaning.

- Chart a new vocabulary word from each study group and talk about the meaning.

DAY 13 Commitment

Focused Instruction

We have discovered so much about many different topics over the last week. Today we are going to show what we have learned! One way to show our learning is by creating a mural. For our class topic, octopuses, we are going to make a mural with many octopuses and facts we have learned. To do our best job making the mural, we need to plan what it will look like.

- Discuss a plan for the mural. Children decide if they each want to make an octopus or work with a partner. Draw a plan on chart paper. This is a whole-class project.

We have decided that our mural will have fact index cards and one octopus that each of you make.

Independent Practice

- Distribute Nonfiction Project Plan (Resource 4.11).

In your reading groups today, you are going to make a plan for your small-group project, just like we made a plan for our whole-class project. You are going to plan what it will look like using the project planning page. Use your plan to draw the pictures and the labels for your poster.

Wrap-Up

- Students share their plan sheets with another group.

DAY 14 Commitment

Focused Instruction

We are going to continue to work on our class mural. The purpose of this mural is to show all of the amazing things we have learned about octopuses. You can each make an octopus to put on the mural. Also, write a fact about octopuses on an index card to add to our mural.

Independent Practice

- Students make their octopuses on paper and each write a fact they learned on an index card.
- While children are working, call a few up at a time to help paint the ocean for the mural.

Wrap-Up

Bring your octopus and index card to the rug. Turn to the person next to you and share the fact you wrote on your card.

DAY 15 Commitment

Focused Instruction

Yesterday we made a wonderful class mural to show what we learned about octopuses. Today you are going to work with your group on your poster to show what you learned about your nonfiction study project. Remember to use your plan sheet to help you.

Independent Practice

- Students use their plan sheets to help make their poster.

Wrap-Up

Tomorrow we are going to celebrate our posters and our learning.

DAY 16 Commitment

Focused Instruction

We have created some wonderful posters that show what we have learned in our nonfiction study groups. Today we are going to celebrate all of our hard work and share our work with our friends in the class.

Independent Practice

- Students rotate through each group sharing their final projects.

Wrap-Up

All of you worked so hard in your nonfiction study groups. Turn to the person next to you and tell him or her one of your favorite parts of studying your nonfiction topic for the last three weeks.

Creating All-About Books: Nonfiction

Why Teach This?

- To teach students how to write nonfiction text.
- To show students how to use what they have learned in nonfiction reading to create a piece of nonfiction writing.

Framing Questions

- How does nonfiction writing look different from fiction writing?
- What features and structures do writers use to write a nonfiction book?

Unit Goals

- Students will create a nonfiction book using nonfiction features.
- Students will show an understanding of the nonfiction genre.
- Students will show evidence of research to get information.
- Students will use graphic organizers to sort and classify information.
- Students will understand drafting, revising, editing, and making a final copy.

Anchor Texts

- *Chameleons Are Cool* by Martin Jenkins
- *I Love Guinea Pigs* by Dick King-Smith
- *My Visit to the Aquarium* by Aliki
- *The Supermarket* by Kathleen Krull
- *Surprising Sharks* by Nicola Davies

Resource Sheets

- Writing Topic (Resource 4.12)
- Big Ideas Plan (Resource 4.13)
- Big Idea/Heading 1 (Resource 4.14)
- Big Idea/Heading 2 (Resource 4.15)
- Big Idea/Heading 3 (Resource 4.16)
- Big Idea/Heading 4 (Resource 4.17)
- Nonfiction Research Questions Homework (Resource 4.18)
- Nonfiction Picture Search Homework (Resource 4.19)

Unit Assessment Creating All-About Books: Nonfiction			GENRE
Student name:	EMERGING	DEVELOPING	INDEPENDENT
Chooses a topic he or she knows a lot about.			
Plans for writing using graphic organizers.			
Understands features of nonfiction and is able to add some to the all-about book.			
Researches a few questions and incorporates them into his or her writing.			
Writes a draft and makes a final copy.			
Shows an understanding of the nonfiction genre.			

Stage of the Unit	Focused Instruction You will	Independent Practice Students will
IMMERSION 1 day	• browse favorite all-about books; review their parts.	• work with a partner to browse all-about books; identify the parts of an all-about book together.
IDENTIFICATION 1 day	• name and identify some possible class topics for writing a nonfiction book.	• identify a topic they want to write about for their nonfiction writing piece.
GUIDED PRACTICE 15 days	• model using a whole-class writing topic, Being a First Grader, and how to use a graphic organizer to list four headings (big ideas) for the book. • using the whole-class writing topic, model how to use graphic organizers to expand on each heading (big idea) with factual information about that particular part (four days, one for each big idea). • using the whole-class writing topic, model how to write a few questions to research the class topic. • model how to begin a first draft using graphic organizers as the plan for the actual writing. • using the whole-class writing topic, model how to continue the drafts. • model how to revise a draft with the whole-class book on chart paper.	• work independently on their nonfiction writing topics using graphic organizers to create headings and break apart each heading into further detail (five days). • use their nonfiction writing topics to write a draft using the graphic organizer to support the writing. • work independently on their nonfiction writing topic by writing a few questions about the topic and researching information to add to the draft. • work independently on their nonfiction books by writing a strong beginning that gets the reader's attention. • work independently on writing drafts of their nonfiction books. • reread to revise their writing using the checklist. • work independently to create an ending for their nonfiction books.

GUIDED PRACTICE (continued)	• model how to write a strong beginning; read the beginning of *Surprising Sharks* and *The Supermarket* and see how Nicola Davis and Kathleen Krull start their books. • model how to write an ending that makes the book sound like it's over. • model how to revise by rereading and how to edit a book. • model how to add pictures or photos and features.	• work independently to place pictures or photos in a book. • work independently to add nonfiction features to their book.
COMMITMENT 4 days	• work on turning a draft into the final copy. • add a cover to the class book. • add features to the class book. • celebrate the finished class book.	• commit to a final copy of the book. • add a cover to the book. • add features to the book. • publish and celebrate books in a nonfiction writing celebration.
TOTAL: 21 DAYS		

Getting Started

The best part of a nonfiction writing unit is hearing the ideas that start swirling around the room. Your students will influence one another, and their ideas are so genuine, so heartfelt, and so thoughtful that your children will inspire one another. Fiona wants to write an all-about book about nursing homes because her grandfather lives in one. Gregory wants to write about hippos after seeing hippos at the zoo and becoming fascinated with them. David wants to write about pianos, as he is an accomplished piano player at age 6.

The class chooses to write together about being a first grader, as by this time of year they all know a lot about being one and want to share what they know with others.

Structures and Routines

Model the writing work to be done during Independent Practice with a whole-class topic chosen with the students. Students should think of something they are all experts in, such as being a first grader or going to school. All of the modeling for the independent writing unit will take place within this whole-class topic.

Partnerships

Students will work with writing partners to help them organize their ideas, write an attention-grabbing beginning, and help with the editing and writing process. Partnerships are an integral component of this unit. Children will need each other's support for many stages of the writing process.

Teaching Materials

The anchor texts from the nonfiction reading unit can be revisited in the writing unit. Choose books that are good models for strong nonfiction writing. It is helpful to provide a double-pocket folder for each child as a nonfiction writing folder. There will be many papers for this unit, and a dedicated folder is a good idea.

Differentiation

As a way to differentiate instruction for this unit, you can have some students create shorter books with fewer big ideas/headings when they write. Often children will be at different parts of the writing process. It is helpful if students have other writing projects going on at the same time. That way, if a student finishes her nonfiction work on a specific day, she may go back to her regular writing folder and work on a different piece of writing. If another system is established to support students who are finished, that will work as well. This will help with classroom management and the ability to confer with the students who need more teacher support during the unit.

Stages of the Unit

Immersion

Students are immersed in nonfiction and recognize the structures and features that make a strong nonfiction book. They are ready to begin to think about planning for writing their own nonfiction piece.

Identification

Students will work on choosing a topic for their nonfiction books while the class focuses on choosing a topic for the class book. Students should choose topics they already know a lot about in order to make the writing process easier.

Guided Practice

This is the one time during the first-grade year when students will go through the entire writing process, from planning with graphic organizers to drafting and creating a final piece. For students with fine motor issues, you may decide that writing only one draft of the book is sufficient.

Commitment

This is the time for children to edit and revise the final copy of their nonfiction book. They will work on placement of pictures, adding features, and making a collage cover. They will finish with a writing celebration, sharing work in a festive fashion, with families present when possible.

Assessment

The assessment for this unit will take place while conferring with groups and taking notes during whole-class instruction. Here are guiding questions for conferences in this unit:

- What are some things you already know about this topic?
- How does this big idea fit into your topic?
- Can you tell me more about that?

- Can you put the book in a sequence (or order) that makes sense?
- Can you use webs to organize information?
- Will your beginning get the reader's attention?

Day-by-Day Lessons

DAY 1 Immersion

Focused Instruction

We have been doing a lot of work in nonfiction reading to recognize the structures and features of nonfiction books. Today we're going to get ready to write our own nonfiction all-about books. Before we pick our topics, we're going to review the parts of an all-about book.

- Browse favorite all-about books.
- Review the features of an all-about book.

Independent Practice

Today you are going to work with a partner to look through some all-about books together. See if you can identify the same features that we looked at. Are there different features in your book?

- Students browse all-about books with a partner.

Wrap-Up

Let's share some of the features we found in our all-about books.

DAY 2 Identification

Focused Instruction

When writers write, they choose topics they know a lot about and can live with for a long time. Let's think about a topic we could write together as a class. What is something we all know a lot about?

- Chart with students some ideas for a class topic to write about.
- Choose a topic with the class.

Independent Practice

- Distribute Writing Topic (Resource 4.12).

Today you are going to think of four possible topics for your own nonfiction book. You can record these topics on your Writing Topic sheet. After you list them, you are going to free-write to help you decide which topic to write about. If the topic is easy to write about it may be a good one to choose. If it feels too hard, then you need to choose a different one from your list.

- Students will free-write on a topic from the sheet.

Wrap-Up

Today we chose a topic for our class nonfiction book and our own nonfiction book. Tomorrow we will begin to get ready for our writing. Turn to the person next to you and share the topic you chose and why you chose that topic to write about.

DAY 3 Guided Practice

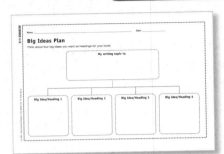

Focused Instruction

- Distribute the Big Ideas Plan (Resource 4.13).

One thing writers do is plan their writing. We are going to spend the next few days planning for our writing to make it easier. A plan helps us to organize our ideas and know what to write. Writers often use webs to sort out their topics. The web I gave you will help us to think about our topic: Being a First Grader. Let's think about four headings that would match our topic. Remember, a heading is a big idea that would be at the top of our page when we write our nonfiction book.

Independent Practice

Your writing work today is to think of four big ideas connected to your topic that will later become headings for your book. For example, for our class book, we picked the first day of school, reading and writing, specials (gym, art, music, and library), and our classroom. Use your plan sheet to think of four big ideas about your topic.

- Students work to come up with four big ideas about their topic and record the ideas on their plan sheets.

Wrap-Up

You worked very hard on coming up with four big ideas for your topic. For the next few days we are going to take each big idea and write some facts about each one. These ideas will then become our headings, and the facts will give us information to put on each page of the book.

DAY 4 Guided Practice

Focused Instruction

Using our idea web from yesterday, we are going to divide our ideas into smaller parts. Again, this will help us with our actual writing. Our first big idea was about the first day of first grade. What are some facts that tell about the first day in first grade?

- List four facts that support the first heading on chart paper.

Independent Practice

- Distribute the Big Idea/Heading 1 (Resource 4.14).

Your independent writing work is to think of facts about your first big idea. For example Christine's nonfiction topic is cats, and her first big idea is what cats eat, so Christine needs to write some different things that cats eat in each of the fact boxes. Record your facts on the big idea plan.

- Students write specific facts about their first big idea on the plan page.

Wrap-Up

Today we used our plan page to write facts about our first big idea. For the next few days we will continue this work, writing facts about all of our big ideas.

DAY 5 Guided Practice

Focused Instruction

Using our big idea web, we are going to divide our next big idea into smaller parts. Again, this will help us with our actual writing. Our second class big idea is reading and writing. What are some facts that tell about reading and writing in our classroom?

- List four facts about the second big idea.

Independent Practice

- Distribute the Big Idea/Heading 2 (Resource 4.15).

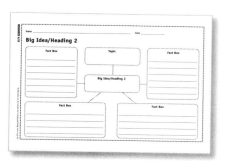

Now you will have the chance to think of facts about your own second big idea. For example John's nonfiction topic is space, and his second big idea is Jupiter. John will list four facts about Jupiter in the fact boxes on his big idea plan.

- Students write specific facts about their second big idea on the plan page.

Wrap-Up

Turn to the person next to you and share your second big idea and the facts you wrote about that idea.

DAY 6 Guided Practice

Focused Instruction

Today we are going to pick the third big idea and divide it into smaller ideas for the planning page. Our third class big idea is specials (gym, art, music, and library). What are some facts that tell about the specials in first grade?

- List four facts about the third class big idea.

Independent Practice

- Distribute the Big Idea/Heading 3 (Resource 4.16).

Your writing work is to think of facts about your third big idea. For example Fiona's topic is nursing homes. Her third big idea is who lives in nursing homes. She will list four facts about who lives in nursing homes.

- Students write specific facts about their third big idea on the plan page.

Wrap-Up

Today we worked on our third big idea. Tomorrow we will begin to work on our fourth big idea.

DAY 7 Guided Practice

Focused Instruction

Our fourth big idea is our classroom. What are some facts we can put in the fact boxes about our classroom? Maybe we can tell about the different parts of the classroom and the way the classroom is set up.

- List four facts about the fourth big idea.

Independent Practice

- Distribute the Big Idea/Heading 4 (Resource 4.17).

Your writing work today is to think of facts about your fourth big idea. For example, Sean's nonfiction book is about pizza. His fourth big idea is how to make pizza. His fact boxes will provide information about this.

- Students write specific facts about their fourth big idea on the plan page.

Wrap-Up

Today we finished breaking down our fourth and last big idea. Turn to the person next to you and share how this went for you.

DAY 8 Guided Practice

Focused Instruction

We all picked nonfiction topics that we feel passionate about and know a lot about. While we were making our webs, we discovered some things that we do not yet know about our topics. One way to get new information about our topics is to ask questions and research the answers, just like we did in our nonfiction reading study groups.

- Think of four questions about the class topic with students.
- Write the four questions on chart paper.

Independent Practice

- Distribute the Nonfiction Research Questions Homework (Resource 4.18).

Today think of four questions you want to find out about your topic. Remember, your four questions need to be specifically about your own nonfiction topic. Write your four questions on the research homework sheet. For the next few nights, you will research the answers to your questions.

- Students will use the research homework sheet to write their questions. The sheet will be sent home and is to be returned on Day 11.

Wrap-Up

Today we wrote some questions that we have about our topics. Turn to the person next to you and share one of the questions you wrote about your topic.

DAY 9 Guided Practice

Focused Instruction

We have done such a good job planning that we are now ready to start working on our first draft. This is really exciting. The first copy of our writing is called a draft. All authors write a draft first and then fix it up to make it ready for the world to read. We are going to do the same thing to make our nonfiction writing the best it can be.

- Model using the web on the first big idea plan sheet to help with ideas, and then turn notes into a page of writing.

Independent Practice

Your writing work today is to use draft paper and write the first page of your book. To do this, you will need your plan sheet with the first big idea on it. This sheet will help you think about what to write. You can use the facts on your web to help you. You can also add to those facts and put your voice into the piece of writing. Remember, your plan sheet for the first big idea is there to help you with your writing. Make sure you use it!

- Students begin to write drafts using their webs to support their writing.

Wrap-Up

Today we worked on writing the first page of our drafts. For the next few days we will continue to work on our writing. Remember that we made our webs to help us figure out what to write about our topics.

DAY 10 Guided Practice

Focused Instruction

We are going to continue drafting. Using our web for page two, let's write about reading and writing. We can use our web to help us with the facts, but we should add more to make the writing interesting.

- Model using the second plan sheet to write the next page of the class book together.

Independent Practice

Your writing work today is to use your second big idea web and draft your second page using draft paper. Again, make sure you use your plan sheet to help you!

- Students continue to write drafts using their webs to support their writing.

Wrap-Up

Turn to the person next to you and share how writing your draft has been going so far.

DAY 11 Guided Practice

Focused Instruction

We have been working hard on our nonfiction writing drafts and today we are going to work on our third page using big idea number three. Our class topic for the third big idea is specials. If we look back at our web, we can see that we listed only the names of the specials in first grade: art, music, gym, and library. So, for our draft we will definitely want to add some information about each special to make the writing interesting for the reader.

Independent Practice

Take out your web for your third big idea and write as much as you can, adding to your facts on draft paper.

- Students continue to write drafts using their webs to support their writing.

Wrap-Up

You are all getting better and better at writing your drafts. Tomorrow you are going to finish up with the fourth big idea.

(Note: Children will be bringing back their research homework today. Have them put it in their nonfiction folders to refer to on Day 13.)

DAY 12 Guided Practice

Focused Instruction

We are now ready to work on our fourth and final draft page. We will continue to use the web page with the big ideas and facts to help us. Our fourth big idea is our classroom, so let's use our plan sheet to help us write more for our first draft.

Independent Practice

Your writing work today is to finish up with your last draft page, draft page number four. Remember to use your plan sheet to help with your ideas and add more to make your writing sound good and make sense.

- Students continue to write drafts using their webs to support their writing.

Wrap-Up

You are now done with the meat of your book—the middle of your drafts. We still need to add a beginning and ending. We will continue this work over the next week and create the rest of our all-about books.

DAY 13 Guided Practice

Focused Instruction

Many of you have already finished your drafts and some of you are still working. Writers always reread what they wrote to make sure it sounds right and makes sense. Writers also make corrections in their writing to make it sound better.

- Model revising by making changes to the whole-class book on chart paper.

Independent Practice

If you are finished with your draft, your writing work today is to reread your writing and see if it makes sense and sounds right. If you are not done with your draft, today's writing work is to finish it up!

- Students work on rereading and revising or finishing up their drafts.

Wrap-Up

Now we are all ready to add more to our writing. Tomorrow we will look at our research questions from home and see if we can find a place to put them into our writing.

- Send home the Nonfiction Picture Search Homework (Resource 4.19) and tell students it's due by Day 17.

DAY 14 Guided Practice

Focused Instruction

We have finally finished our rough draft using our webs to help us with our writing. Today we are going to look back at our research homework and see if we can use any of the ideas in our writing. Your questions and answers may fit under one of the headings you have already written. If it does not, then we can add a page at the end with the new information or facts we have found.

Independent Practice

Now it's time to reread your draft to a writing partner. As you read, make sure your writing makes sense. Then ask your partner to help you find a place to put the new information you found when you researched. You may find that it fits in perfectly, or you may find that it needs to go at the end of your book.

Wrap-Up

Some of you found places in your book where you could easily fit the research you found at home. Others had a hard time finding a place for it. If you had a hard time, you can put a fact sheet at the end of your all-about book.

DAY 15 Guided Practice

Focused Instruction

Now that we have finished our drafts, we are going to write the most important part, the beginning! A good beginning is really important because the beginning is what gets the reader's attention and makes him or her want to read on. There are many ways to get a reader's attention. Remember the beginning of the book Surprising Sharks *by Nicola Davis? She sets the scene by using a variety of punctuation and print types, and she also uses noise words.*

- Review beginnings that get the reader's attention using a variety of books including *The Supermarket* by Kathleen Krull, *Surprising Sharks* by Nicola Davies, and other books that have strong beginnings.

- Create a chart like the one below to show the qualities of great beginnings:

Great Beginnings get the reader's attention by:
- using a variety of punctuation
- making you laugh
- repeating something in the last line that was stated in the first
- using different types of print (bold, italic, small words, big words)
- putting in interesting facts
- capturing the author's voice
- using noise words (onomatopoeia)
- asking a question
- describing the setting

Independent Practice

Your writing work today is to think of a great beginning for your nonfiction book. You can use any of the ways listed on our Great Beginnings chart to get the reader's attention, or you can use another technique that you invent to get people excited about your book.

Wrap-Up

Turn to the person next to you and share how you decided to get the reader's attention for the beginning of your book.

DAY 16 Guided Practice

Focused Instruction

Now that we have the beginning for our book, we can work on writing the ending. An ending is what makes the book sound like it is over. It can sum up the ideas written in the rest of the book. Let's think about our class book, Being a First Grader. What would be a good way to end this book? Turn to the person next to you and talk about what would make this book sound like it is over. Now as a class let's discuss what would work for the end of our class book.

- As a class, decide on a good ending. Here is what this class decided: "Now you have learned about all of the fun things we do in first grade. We hope that you like it when you go to first grade. If you have already been to first grade, then good luck in the other grades!"

Independent Practice

Today you will write an ending for your all-about book that tells the reader the book is over.

- Students work on creating an ending.

Wrap-Up

All of you wrote endings that let your reader know your book is over. Turn to the person next to you and share the ending of your book.

DAY 17 Guided Practice

Focused Instruction

We have spent the last few weeks working on the drafts of our nonfiction books. Today we are going to edit and revise our writing. We will make sure our writing makes sense, that it sounds right, and we will fix some of our spelling words.

- Model rereading and editing with whole-class book.

Independent Practice

While you are waiting for me to confer with you, please sit with your writing partner and go through your writing together to see if you can do some of your own editing and revising. Check for capital letters, punctuation, and your spelling words.

- Give students an editing checklist like the one below. Students will read through their writing, looking for the following points to edit. After they correct these points, they will check off the spaces on the checklist.

Name _____ Date _____
- ❏ I used proper punctuation at the end of my sentences.
- ❏ I used mostly lowercase letters in my writing.
- ❏ I used uppercase letters at the beginning of a sentence.
- ❏ I checked the word wall words.
- ❏ I checked my personal spelling words.

- Confer with students, helping them to revise and edit their writing. Allow students to use a colored pen to note where changes need to be made.

Wrap-Up

Many of you worked hard with your writing partners to work on revising and editing. Remember you can also use your colored pens to work on this. That way, you can see all of the changes on your drafts. Before we finish, let's briefly share our picture homework with our writing partner to see what we gathered.

DAY 18 Commitment

Focused Instruction

Now it is time to write the final copies of our books. I know you are so excited! One of the things I noticed in all of the nonfiction books we have read over the last month is that the pictures are in all different places on the page. As the author of your own book, you can decide where the pictures go and where the writing goes. The writing part will be easy. Copy your draft onto the final pages using your BEST handwriting. This may take a few days, but your final copy will look great and you will be ready to share your nonfiction information with others.

Independent Practice

Your writing work for the next few days is to work on your final piece of writing. First look through the pictures you brought in and decide which ones you will use. Then decide where your pictures will go on each page and make sure they match the words. When you've decided how to use the pictures, write the words on each page.

Wrap-Up

- Students share how they decided to place their pictures on the final drafts.

DAY 19 Commitment

Focused Instruction

As we have learned, some nonfiction books have a table of contents, glossary, index, and other features. Decide if you would like to add any features to your finished book, including a table of contents. If you add a table of contents, remember to put your heading on the line and the page number where that heading starts. You may want to talk to your writing partner to decide the best places in your book to add features.

- Model adding features to the whole-class book.

Independent Practice

Continue to work on your writing, adding any of the features we have learned about.

- Students continue to work on the final copy.

Wrap-Up

I noticed that many of you used a lot of different features, including a table of contents, labels, photographs, and diagrams. These will make all of our nonfiction books more interesting to read and clearer for the reader.

DAY 20 Commitment

Focused Instruction

If we look at any of our favorite nonfiction books, they each have great pictures on the cover. One of the ways that authors or illustrators make covers is by doing a collage. A collage is when you paste pictures and writing onto another piece of paper.

Independent Practice

Your writing work today is to make a collage cover. You can use any of the leftover pictures you have from your picture homework, or you can draw some new pictures for the cover.

- Confer with students helping them with placement of the pictures and the title on the covers of their books.

Wrap-Up

Share your cover with the person next to you.

DAY 21 Commitment

Focused Instruction

We have all worked so hard on our all-about books. Today we are going to celebrate our work with a nonfiction writing celebration!

Independent Practice

I am going to put you in a group with three other children. In your group, your job is to do two things. First listen to each other's nonfiction book. Second make a comment about your friend's book. Your comment can be something you learned or something you liked about the book. Each writer in your group should hear three positive comments about his or her book.

Wrap-Up

Turn to someone who was not in your sharing group. Tell them one thing from one of your friends' books that you learned or a part that you liked. Make sure to tell them the title of the book as well!

Re-seeing, Rethinking, Revision

These next two units, Developing Print Strategies and Enhancing Our Writing, are linked by virtue of the fact that they are all about re-seeing. What a perfect time to talk with your students about the act of re-seeing. It is winter, and first-grade classrooms are alive with the books and conversations of the months that have passed. You have baskets full of cherished read-alouds. And first graders love to reread. They love to know what comes next, and can listen to a favorite read-aloud over and over. They are also working hard when they reread and when they listen again to familiar text. The work of their rereading is important; it is about building stamina, about revisiting ideas, and about focusing more on other elements besides what comes next, such as their interpretation of character or their awareness of the setting and dialogue. The act of rereading is a powerful one, both for comprehension and for decoding. Effective readers revisit text and have strategies for approaching difficult passages. This reading unit is about the act of rereading to master print and to delve deeper into comprehension. In writing, our parallel is revision. There, too, our first-grade writers are learning the power of re-seeing. What better learning for this most observant age? They are noticing everything—the streak of color in the sky in the early morning, the texture of your hand. Revision for them is a natural; they love to linger on their fresh words, and they adore hearing one another's writing. Their worlds are all new, and re-seeing is everything made new, again.

Developing Print Strategies: Readers Reread and Revise

CONVENTIONS

Why Teach This?
- To help students become problem solvers as they read.
- To encourage students to check for meaning when rereading.
- To help students learn that reading is a meaning-making process.

Framing Questions
- Why do readers reread parts of a book?
- How do readers check for understanding during reading?

Unit Goals
- Students will review strategies to figure out an unknown word.
- Students will reread a sentence after using a word-solving strategy.
- Students will stop during reading to make sure they know what is happening in a book.
- Students will quickly recap a story during reading to make sure they know what is happening in a book.
- Students will decide what to reread if they don't know what is happening in a book.
- Students will revise their thinking about a book as their understanding grows.

Anchor Texts

- *Amazing Grace* by Mary Hoffman
- *Bigmama's* by Donald Crews
- *A Weekend With Wendell* by Kevin Henkes
- *Yoko* by Rosemary Wells

Unit Assessment Developing Print Strategies: Readers Reread and Revise		CONVENTIONS	
Student name:	EMERGING	DEVELOPING	INDEPENDENT
Uses strategies to figure out an unknown word.			
Rereads sentences after using a word-attack strategy.			
Stops during reading to make sure he or she knows what is happening in a book.			
Retells a story to make sure he or she knows what is happening in a book.			
Decides what to reread if he or she doesn't know what is happening in a book.			
Revises his or her thinking about a book as understanding grows.			

Stage of the Unit	Focused Instruction You will	Independent Practice Students will
IMMERSION 2 days	• read excerpt from *Bigmama's*; model getting stuck on a word that you don't know; after trying out a word-attack strategy, reread the whole sentence to make sure it makes sense; ask students what they noticed about what you did. • read *Amazing Grace*; model reading a book aloud and not following the story or understanding what is happening; think aloud about how readers reread and rethink before reading on; ask students what they noticed about what you did.	• read with a partner, noticing any reading strategies used (word attack, rereading, or rethinking).

IDENTIFICATION 1 day	• revisit the chart of strategies that readers use to help them read (from the fall Print Strategies unit, see page 27); start a new chart, "What do good readers do while reading?"	• practice the word-attack strategies from the Print Strategies chart; experiment with rereading during Independent Practice, noticing what they chose to reread.
GUIDED PRACTICE 5 days	• read *Bigmama's*; model how readers reread a sentence after they have used a word-attack strategy, asking "Does that make sense?" to see if the word works. • use *Amazing Grace* to model how readers stop during reading to make sure they know what is happening in the book. • use *Bigmama's* to model how readers quickly recap the story in their mind during reading to make sure they know what is happening; use beginning, middle, and end to guide the quick recap during reading. • read *Yoko*; model how readers decide what to reread if they can't figure out what is happening in a book. • read *A Weekend With Wendell*; model how readers revise their thinking about a book as their understanding changes and grows.	• reread a sentence after they've used a word-attack strategy, asking themselves, "Does that make sense?" • stop during reading to make sure they know what is happening in the book. • quickly recap the story in their mind during reading to make sure they know what is happening. • decide whether they need to reread if they don't know what is happening in a book. • revise their thinking about a book as their understanding changes and grows.
COMMITMENT 1 day	• use *Yoko* to model how to decide which rereading strategy to use when reading a book; think aloud throughout modeling to emphasize how readers decide when to reread.	• reflect on which rereading strategies are most helpful when reading independently.
TOTAL: 9 DAYS		

Enhancing Our Writing: Revision Strategies

STRATEGY

Why Teach This?

- To teach students revision strategies they can use to improve their writing.
- To demonstrate how writers reread and revise their writing many times before it is finished.

Framing Questions

- What is revision?
- How do writers revise their work?

Unit Goals

- Students will identify a writing piece they want to revise.
- Students will use sticky notes to revise words in a writing piece.
- Students will use sticky notes to add or change sentences in a writing piece.
- Students will visualize their story to add details to their writing.
- Students will add details to their illustrations to strengthen their story.

Anchor Texts

- *Some Things Change* by Mary Murphy

Unit Assessment Enhancing Our Writing: Revision Strategies			**STRATEGY**
Student name:	**EMERGING**	**DEVELOPING**	**INDEPENDENT**
Identifies a piece of writing he or she wants to revise.			
Uses sticky notes to revise or add words.			
Uses sticky notes to add or change sentences in a writing piece.			
Visualizes his or her story to add details.			
Adds details to illustrations to revise a writing piece.			

Stage of the Unit	Focused Instruction You will	Independent Practice Students will
IMMERSION 2 days	• read *Some Things Change*; explain that our own writing changes; read a piece of writing that you've written and think aloud about the changes that you might like to make to revise the piece. • show a writing piece from your writer's notebook that is in the process of revision (sticky notes added, colored pencil marks, pages taped on); ask students what they notice about the writing piece.	• reread writing pieces from their writer's notebook or folder; choose one they would like to revise, and share it with a partner, describing what changes they might make. • choose a writing piece that they want to revise and use a sticky note to mark one part they would like to change.

IDENTIFICATION 1 day	• start a class chart, "How Do Writers Revise Their Writing?" and explain that you will use this chart to list the ways that writers go back and make changes on their writing; list step one: Writers reread the piece they will revise two times, once in their head and once aloud.	• reread the writing piece they chose to revise two times, once in their head and once aloud.
GUIDED PRACTICE 6 days	• model how writers use sticky notes to revise words in a writing piece, thinking carefully about word choice; demonstrate on the writing piece you chose to revise, emphasizing that writers reread the change to make sure it makes sense. • model how writers use sticky notes to change sentences in a writing piece, thinking about how a sentence helps tell your story. • model how writers visualize their story after they read it to add details to their writing. • model how writers use sticky notes to add on to their writing or insert sentences. • model how writers add on to their story by adding paper with additional information; show writers where these materials will be located in the writing area. • model how writers look carefully at their illustrations to add details in their drawings.	• use sticky notes to revise words in the writing piece they chose; reread their changes to make sure they make sense. • use sticky notes to change sentences in their writing pieces, thinking about how the sentences help tell a story. • visualize their story after they read it to identify details they want to add to their story. • use sticky notes to add on to their writing or insert sentences. • add on to their stories by adding new material on paper. • look carefully at their illustrations to add details to their drawings.
COMMITMENT 1 day	• share your original writing piece with the class and show the changes you made; describe why you decided to make the changes you did; read the revised writing piece aloud.	• meet with a partner to describe the changes they made to their writing piece and why they made them, then read their revised piece to their partner.
TOTAL: 10 DAYS		

Versatile Readers, Versatile Writers

Your students are trying on many hats. They are learning how to write fiction, nonfiction, and very soon, poetry. As this season draws to an end, we help our students create connections across genres—naming the containers for their ideas. Spring is approaching, and with it students' newfound confidence in themselves as fluent readers and writers in the world, magicians, poets, researchers, novelists. All is possible.

Making Meaning: Connecting Across Genres

STRATEGY

Why Teach This?

- To identify and compare different genres—fiction, nonfiction, poetry, signs/letters.
- To expose students to the similarities and differences across genres.
- To encourage students to make connections across genres.

Framing Question

- How do readers compare different kinds of texts?

Unit Goals

- Students will identify fiction, nonfiction, poetry, and signs/letters.
- Students will compare different genre qualities and features.
- Students will make connections across genres.

Anchor Texts

- *A Book About Bears* by Mel Berger
- *Brown Bear, Brown Bear, What Do You See?* by Eric Carle and Bill Martin, Jr.
- *Fish Eyes* by Mia Ocean
- *Hello Fish!* by Sylvia Earle
- *I Read Signs* by Tana Hoban
- *The Rainbow Fish* by Marcus Pfister
- *Swimmy* by Leo Lionni
- *What's It Like to Be a Fish?* by Wendy Pfeffer

Unit Assessment Making Meaning: Connecting Across Genres			STRATEGY
Student name:	EMERGING	DEVELOPING	INDEPENDENT
Identifies fiction, nonfiction, poetry, signs/letters.			
Identifies and compares different genre features.			
Discusses features and connections with a partner.			

Stage of the Unit	Focused Instruction You will	Independent Practice Students will
IMMERSION 4 days	• read *Swimmy* and talk about what students notice in the text (story, characters, illustrations). • read *What's It Like to Be a Fish?* and talk about what students notice in the text (facts, no story, no characters, information). • read *Fish Eyes* and talk about what students notice in the text (white space, how the words are positioned). • read *I Read Signs* and talk about what students notice in the text (no characters, no story, simple sentences).	• browse different book baskets labeled "fiction," "nonfiction," "poetry," and "signs/letters." • read fiction texts with a partner and discuss what they notice. • read a poem with a partner and discuss what they notice about white space and the position of words. • read nonfiction texts with a partner and discuss what they notice.
IDENTIFICATION 1 day	• create a chart that compares the identifying features of each text: fiction, nonfiction, poetry, and signs/letters; use the read-aloud books to list features that describe each genre.	• identify features from the chart in the books they read independently; discuss with a partner one unique feature they noticed in a book they read.
GUIDED PRACTICE 4 days	• compare a fiction and a nonfiction book with a similar theme or topic; place a sticky note on one feature difference between the fiction and the nonfiction texts, then ask students how they look different. • compare a fiction and a nonfiction book with similar theme or topic; place a sticky note on one difference in the writing between fiction and nonfiction texts and ask students how they sound different. • model comparing two different texts and making a connection between them; introduce the phrase "This reminds me of" to compare the texts. • model using the phrase "I notice" to compare two texts with a partner; model using this phrase to draw connections between two texts.	• work with a partner to compare a fiction and a nonfiction text with a similar theme or topic and use a sticky note to mark a feature difference they found. • work with a partner to compare a fiction and a nonfiction text with a similar theme or topic, and then use a sticky note to mark a difference in the writing between the two texts. • compare two different texts with a partner and use the phrase "This reminds me of" to compare the texts. • use the phrase "I notice" to compare two texts (of their choice) with a partner.
COMMITMENT 1 day	• compare two texts that you read in this unit and write one connection between the texts.	• compare two texts that they read in this unit and write one connection between the texts.
TOTAL: 10 DAYS		

EARLY FALL

LATE FALL

WINTER

SPRING

From Winter to Spring

The winter comes to a close. Our students have learned so much during this season. They have discovered print strategies that will really work for them and they have revised their work in new ways. Their growing understanding of genre is leading to exciting new work in both reading and writing. They are now ready for the spring season during which they will continue to build their fluency and stamina in both reading and writing.

Chapter 5

SPRING

The First Grader as Fluent Reader and Writer

"Together we will plant. Together we will build. Together we will harvest."
—from *The Legend of Mexicatl* by Jo Harper

How far your first graders have come! Together you have planted the seeds for fluency in reading and writing, built reading and writing partnerships, and harvested new ideas together as readers. Now we enter our final season of learning together, with special emphasis on fluency throughout the season. We send our students joyously and confidently off to second grade with a strong foundation as readers and writers.

SPRING UNITS

SPOTLIGHT on Conventions

- Sounding Like Readers: Fluency and Phrasing
- Using Fluency and Phrasing to Enhance Our Writing

As first-grade teachers, we often either dread teaching conventions because they feel so detached from the liveliness of our students' literacy experiences or we cram in lots of instruction in concentrated periods of time, worried that we are not covering it all before they move on to the next grade. The Complete 4 approach advocates finding a middle ground. We are not going to teach conventions in isolation (although we do advocate regular word-work time for practice with patterns and strategies), nor are we going to ignore them. Instead, we are going to carefully place conventions instruction where it belongs: alongside students' authentic work. We celebrate language, punctuation, and grammar in ways that respect and give dignity to the way first graders are coming to print. The writer Eudora Welty recalled her first glimpse as a child of the alphabet inside her storybooks and how magical the swirls and curves of each letter seemed. Let us capture that magic in units on conventions.

We tend to sprinkle fluency lessons in with our bigger units of study or depend on our guided reading groups to accommodate our need to address the issue with our children. But there is so much we can talk to out students about in terms of how to build fluency. We can demonstrate through the read-aloud how readers use punctuation, print type, and phrasing to read smoothly. We can talk with our students about how they build their capacities in their own reading. This unit coalesces these lessons into ideas children can understand and use in their independent reading.

See pages 62–72 in *The Complete 4 for Literacy* for more guidelines for this component.

Pam Allyn

Sounding Like Readers: Fluency and Phrasing

CONVENTIONS

Why Teach This?

- To help students understand how punctuation, print type, and phrasing change how we read.
- To teach students how reading fluently helps with comprehension.
- To show students how reading should sound.

Framing Questions

- How do readers use punctuation, print type, and phrasing to read fluently?
- How does reading fluently help with comprehension?

Unit Goals

- Students will recognize the sound of "smooth" reading instead of "robot" reading.
- Students will practice reading like they talk.
- Students will learn how reading fluently helps us with comprehension.
- Students will understand phrasing and how we read phrases together.
- Students will become expressive readers.
- Students will use punctuation, phrases, and print type to change the way we read.

Anchor Texts

- *Bark, George* by Jules Feiffer (punctuation, print type)
- *Has Anyone Seen William?* by Bob Graham (punctuation, print type, phrasing)
- *The Hungry Giant* by Joy Cowley (punctuation, print type)
- *I Lost My Bear* by Jules Feiffer (punctuation, print type, phrasing)
- *Knuffle Bunny* by Mo Willems (punctuation, print type, phrasing)
- *Muncha! Muncha! Muncha!* by Candace Fleming (punctuation, print type, phrasing)
- *Wolf!* by Becky Bloom (punctuation, print type)

Resource Sheets

- Reading With Expression and Fluency Homework (Resource 5.1)
- Fluency Unit Assessment (Resource 5.2)

Unit Assessment Sounding Like Readers: Fluency and Phrasing			CONVENTIONS
Student name:	EMERGING	DEVELOPING	INDEPENDENT
Identifies varied punctuation.			
Understands how punctuation changes the way we read.			
Identifies phrases.			
Understands how phrases are read together.			
Identifies varied print type.			
Understands how varied print type changes the voice as we read.			
Practices reading smoothly.			
Understands how fluent reading affects comprehension.			

Stage of the Unit	Focused Instruction You will	Independent Practice Students will
IMMERSION 1 day	• show students varied punctuation and print type (this will not be new to them). • model with *Wolf!* by Becky Bloom how fluent reading sounds.	• look at a book with a partner and put a sticky note in a place where they find varied punctuation and print type.
IDENTIFICATION 1 day	• identify types of punctuation, varied print, and phrases.	• sit with a partner and look at a book together to find varied punctuation, print type, and phrases, and put a sticky note on those spots.

GUIDED PRACTICE
8 days
	• read *Bark, George* and model model how periods and commas change our reading.
	• use *Has Anyone Seen William?* to model how questions mark change.
	• use *Muncha! Muncha! Muncha!* to model how exclamation points change our reading.
	• use *Bark, George* to model how ellipses change our reading.
	• use *Wolf!* and *The Hungry Giant* to model how quotation marks change our reading.
	• use *I Lost My Bear* to model how bold letters, italics, and big and small words change our reading.
	• read *Knuffle Bunny* and model what a phrase sounds like.
		• practice reading independently while doing the following:
		  • stopping at a period
		  • pausing at a comma
		  • raising the voice when there is an exclamation point
		  • adding excitement to the voice when there is an exclamation point
		  • using print type to show excitement and make the voice get louder and quieter
		  • changing the voice to sound like someone is talking
		  • practice reading in phrases
		  • reading with fluency

COMMITMENT 1 day	• reflect on how reading now sounds different.	• reflect on how a partner reads to them and decide what print type, punctuation, or phrases they are using to read.
TOTAL: 11 DAYS		

Getting Started

Much of this unit is modeled during the read-aloud and shared reading time. Children practice what they have learned during Independent Practice. At the end of each lesson, we come back and reflect on our learning or share with others how our reading has changed now that we have this newfound knowledge about conventions.

Partnerships

Partnerships are flexible throughout the year, depending on the purpose. During this unit, partnerships are homogenous so students can read books together that are at their level. You may want to prepare some bags of books for students, making sure to include books that have the punctuation they need to find so that you know they will be able to practice the Focused Instruction lesson.

Teaching Materials

There are so many picture books that are elegantly written and convey the use of conventions in a beautiful manner. We have listed some of our favorites for you here.

The books are marked as to which part of the study as follows:

Title of Book	Author	Models Punctuation, Print Type and/or Phrasing
Bark, George	Jules Feiffer	punctuation, print type
CDB	William Steig	punctuation
Diamond Life	Charles Smith	print type, phrasing
Eats, Shoots and Leaves: Why Commas Really Do Make a Difference (children's version)	Lynne Truss	punctuation, phrasing
Good Boy, Fergus	David Shannon	punctuation, print type
Has Anyone Here Seen William?	Bob Graham	punctuation, print type, phrasing
I Lost My Bear	Jules Feiffer	punctuation, print type, phrasing
I'm Not Bobby	Jules Feiffer	punctuation, print type
Knuffle Bunny	Mo Willems	punctuation, print type, phrasing
Muncha! Muncha! Muncha!	Candace Fleming	punctuation, print type, phrasing
Night Noises	Mem Fox	punctuation, print type
The Night I Followed the Dog	Nina Laden	punctuation, print type
No, David!	David Shannon	punctuation, print type
Nocturne	Jane Yolen	punctuation, print type
Pigeon Series	Mo Willems	punctuation, print type
Rattletrap Car	Phyllis Root	punctuation, print type, phrasing
The Recess Queen	Alexis O'Neil	punctuation, print type
Welcome, Precious	Nikki Grimes	punctuation
Wolf!	Becky Bloom	punctuation, print type
Yo! Yes?	Chris Raschka	punctuation, print type

These texts all use punctuation, capitalization, print type, and phrasing both conventionally and unconventionally. All of these books are good examples of how conventions change the way we read and how they can affect our fluency and comprehension.

Jules Feiffer's book *Bark, George* can be used to demonstrate how ellipses show that more is coming and create a sense of anticipation. In Mo Willems's Pigeon books, the punctuation drives the storyline and determines the mood of the books. Another favorite is *Wolf!* by Becky Bloom. In this clever book, a wolf is learning how to read and spends much time working on his reading "style," showing how important it is that we use punctuation to drive our reading and help with our comprehension.

Some great Big Books for this unit include *Move Over!* and *The Hungry Giant*, both by Joy Cowley, and *Who's in the Shed?* by Brenda Parkes.

Stages of the Unit

Immersion

Children will look through books and notice what they see. They will be looking for different types of punctuation and various print types. Send a letter home to parents, encouraging them to support your work.

Dear Parents,

We are working on a unit in reading workshop called Sounding Like Readers. The purpose of this unit is to help children read fluently and with expression. Over time a child's fluency is directly related to his or her comprehension. The content of this unit includes:

- recognizing the sound of "smooth" reading instead of "robot" reading

- reading like we talk

- learning how reading fluently helps us with comprehension

- understanding "phrasing" and how we read phrases together (instead of saying "peanut-butter-and-jelly" we say "peanut butter and jelly" as a phrase, or "at-the-park" is really "at the park")

- being an expressive reader

- using punctuation, phrases, and print type to change the way we read (big letters we say in a loud voice, while little letters we say in a softer voice)

In order to support our work, please emphasize the sound of smooth reading with your child. Our inflection and expression is what makes a story so wonderful to read and listen to.

Warmly,

Above is a letter you can send to parents to help support their children's learning in this unit.

Identification

Students will become familiar with the names of specific punctuation. Even if they do not fully understand the use of each symbol, each one should be named and noticed so that the language of conventions becomes familiar.

This unit will focus on periods, ellipses, parentheses, quotation marks, question marks, exclamation points, commas, and with some groups, the colon and/or semicolon.

Guided Practice

Students begin to search for punctuation, print type, and phrases in their reading, and practice changing their voices to match the punctuation, print type, and phrases they read.

Commitment

As first graders listen to their partners, they guess the punctuation or type of print their partner is reading. Students will be reminded that this is the new way we will read to make it interesting and help us understand the books we read.

Day-by-Day Lessons

DAY 1 Immersion

Focused Instruction

As readers, we want to understand what we are reading. If we are reading aloud, we want others to follow along and understand as well. Punctuation, print type, and phrases all change the way we read. Over the next two weeks we are going to notice and experiment with how our voices sound different when we pay attention to punctuation and phrasing as we read.

Independent Practice

Your reading work today is to look through the books on your table. Put a sticky note wherever you see some punctuation or types of print that stand out.

- Students browse books for places to put sticky notes.

Wrap-Up

Let's talk about some of the punctuation and print type we found today as we were browsing through books. What did you find?

- Chart what students found during Independent Practice.

DAY 2 Identification

Focused Instruction

Yesterday we looked through some books that have different kinds of print and punctuation. Punctuation tells us when to slow down and when to stop. Certain punctuation marks, like the exclamation point, remind us to show excitement when we read out loud so we can hear what is on the page. Print type also changes how we read. The print type can make our voice get louder, quieter, and show anger and other emotions. Phrases are words that go together so they make us read like we talk, with fluency, instead of like a robot.

Independent Practice

Your reading work today is to look at the books on a different table. Again, put a sticky note on any of the things we have talked about that change how we read. See if you can name some of the punctuation or types of print.

- Students browse books looking for different punctuation and print type.
- Confer with students, helping them to name conventions.

Wrap-Up

What kinds of punctuation and print type did you find today? Turn to the person next to you and share.

DAY 3 Guided Practice

Focused Instruction

- It is helpful to model these lessons with some of the read-alouds mentioned earlier in the chapter. You may choose to use one of the books over and over, or use different books. It is helpful to refer back to familiar read-alouds for the Focused Instruction and model how reading changes based on the punctuation studied on that day. Think about what books your first graders like and what would work best for each lesson.

Focused Instruction

- Create a chart like the one below and share it with students.

Punctuation	
Period .	Ellipsis ...
Comma ,	Quotation Marks " "
Question Mark ?	Colon :
Exclamation point !	Semicolon ;

Over the past two days we skimmed some books looking for punctuation, types of print, and phrasing. We are ready to be punctuation detectives. Remember, a detective is someone who finds something.

The first two things on the chart are the period and the comma. The period tells us when to take a breath at the end of a sentence. If we did not read with periods, the writing would not make sense. The comma is a shorter pause than the period, and when we see it we take a little bit of a breath too, a pause.

- The comma is a very hard concept for first graders, but it is important to introduce it so students begin to become familiar with it.
- Read *Bark, George* to model how periods and commas change our reading.

Independent Practice

When you read with your partner, look for some periods and commas. Put a sticky note in a spot where you used this punctuation to help you read. Practice reading using the periods and commas with your reading partner.

Wrap-Up

I noticed today that many of you were pausing at the commas and taking breaths at the periods. This helps you as a reader and your partner as a listener to follow the story and understand what you are reading and what the author meant. Robert and Christine did a really good job using this punctuation today. They are going to read you the part of the book where they tried changing their voices to match the punctuation.

DAY 4 Guided Practice

Focused Instruction

Let's look at the punctuation chart again. The next mark that I see is the question mark. When you see a question mark it means someone is asking a question. When we see one, our voice goes up. So if I saw the sentence "Do you like pizza?" my voice would go up to show that I am asking a question. Turn to the person next to you and ask them a question, practicing making your voice go up.

- Read *Has Anyone Seen William?* to model how question marks change our reading.

Independent Practice

Meet with your reading partner and place a sticky note next to a place where you see a question mark in your reading. You are a detective looking for question marks.

Wrap-Up

Many of you found question marks. Turn to the person next to you and read the part of your book where you found a question mark. Remember that when you see this mark your voice goes up to show that someone is asking a question.

DAY 5 Guided Practice

Focused Instruction

Another punctuation mark is called an exclamation point or exclamation mark. It looks like a period with a lowercase l above it. When we see an exclamation point, it is usually showing excitement, anger, frustration, happiness, or other strong feelings. Our voice can get louder to show these emotions. Today we are going to practice making our voice sound louder when we see an exclamation point.

- Read *Muncha! Muncha! Muncha!* to model how exclamation points change our reading.

Independent Practice

Today's reading work is to meet with your reading partner and be an exclamation point detective. Put a sticky note in a place where you see an exclamation point. Practice making your voice get louder or sound excited.

Wrap-Up

I am going to ask pairs to show where they found an exclamation point and how their voices changed when they got to this punctuation. Listen carefully to how their voices changed!

- Choose two pairs who found exclamation points and have them share.
- Allow children to use a chart like the one below to post their findings over the last three days.

> We have found punctuation in our reading and in our writing. It changes the way we read and makes stories easier to understand while sounding better. Put your sticky notes under the punctuation marks you found in your reading.
>
> | ! | ? | , |

DAY 6 Guided Practice

Focused Instruction

The next punctuation mark on our chart is called the ellipsis. We have talked about ellipses before. When you see an ellipsis, it means that more is coming on the next page, or something more might happen. It could be that something exciting is happening or that you want the reader to wonder what is next and read on. Remember in Bark, George, *when the doctor reached deep down inside of George and pulled out a . . .*

- Show pages in the book where there is an ellipsis.

Independent Practice

Your reading work today, detectives, is to look for ellipses in your books. You may want to use one of our read-alouds to find one. When you find an ellipsis, put a sticky note on the page and practice reading with your partner. Remember your voice needs to sound like there is more to come when you get to the last word before the ellipsis.

Wrap-Up

There are many great detectives in our classroom! Many of you found ellipses and remembered how to change your voice to show that more is coming. Turn to the partners next to you to share where you found ellipses in your books.

DAY 7 Guided Practice

Focused Instruction

Other marks that we see are called quotation marks, which show that someone is talking. We can also call them talking marks. When we see them, we know that the character in the story is talking. We can change our voice to match the voice that we think this character might have. Remember the book Wolf! *As you can see, when the wolf is talking to the other farm animals there are quotation marks around what he is saying. His voice might sound deep and mean like a wolf, right? Listen to me read it.*

- For this day, partners may use a familiar book or copy of a text that has quotation marks. Students will enjoy changing the tone of their voices for the character speaking and using everything they know about punctuation to read with intonation.

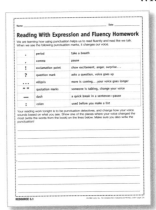

Independent Practice

Your reading work today is to find a spot where there are quotation marks in one of your books. Remember to change your voice to sound like the character that is talking.

Wrap-Up

Today I heard many voices changing when a character was talking. Gregory and Jordi changed their voices to sound like a giant in the book The Hungry Giant *when the giant was talking. They are now going to read that part for you to show you how it sounded.*

- Send home Reading with Expression and Fluency Homework (Resource 5.1) tonight.

DAY 8 Guided Practice

Focused Instruction

- Create a chart like the one below and share with students.

Print type changes the way we read.	
BOLD	Colorful letters
CAPITALS	small and BIG words
Italics	word bubbles

We have spent the last week looking at punctuation and practicing changing our voice to match the punctuation we see. Now we are going to look at another thing that can change how we read. We are going to notice print type. Sometimes in a book, the words look different.

Words can be in bold, capitals, italics, colors, small or big letters, or even in word bubbles. One of the books that has a lot of different print types is I Lost My Bear *by Jules Feiffer. Turn to the person next to you and talk about how your voice would change on the page in* I Lost My Bear *where you see bold, capitals, and word bubbles.*

- Chart with class how they think the reader's voice should change for different types of print.

Independent Practice

Your reading work today is to be print type detectives in your book selections. Practice changing how you read to match the print type. Put a sticky note in the spots where you notice print type and think about how it changes your reading.

Wrap-Up

As I met with you today, I noticed many of you using print type to change your voices. This makes it easier for you and an audience to understand the book. It also helps make the book sound more interesting. Remember to keep trying this as you read.

DAY 9 Guided Practice

Focused Instruction

We are going to spend one more day looking at books to find different print type and punctuation. Today we'll put what we know together and practice reading like we talk to make it interesting for the listener.

- Model fluent reading using print type and punctuation with one of the anchor texts listed earlier in this unit.

Independent Practice

Your reading work today is to be print type detectives. Put a sticky note in a place in a book where you think you and your partner did a really good job using the print type and punctuation to sound like the best readers you can be.

Wrap-Up

Turn to the partners next to you and listen to how they read. See if you can figure out what print type your friends are reading by how they read it, without looking at the book.

DAY 10 Guided Practice

Focused Instruction

- On chart paper, create a list of phrases like the one below.

Phrasing Changes the Way We Read	
peanut butter and jelly	on your hook
in the park	after lunch
through the woods	in the morning
over the mountain	

You have learned so much about punctuation and print type. Today I am going to show you one more thing that helps us read like we talk. Sometimes related groups of words go together in what we call phrases. Here are some examples of phrases: peanut butter and jelly, in the park, over the bridge, through the woods, after lunch, and for my grandmother.

So when I read "peanut butter and jelly," I do not say peanut, butter, and jelly, I say it all together as a phrase, peanut butter and jelly. In one of our favorite books, Knuffle Bunny, *there are many phrases.*

Independent Practice

Your reading work today is to find the phrases in Knuffle Bunny *such as "not so long ago" on the very first page. Practice reading those phrases quickly, like the way we talk. Remember the words in a phrase go together, almost like one word.*

Wrap-Up

Let's list some of the phrases we found in Knuffle Bunny. *Remember, a phrase is made up of words that go together.*

DAY 11 Commitment

Focused Instruction

I am going to read you a piece of my writing. I want you to listen carefully and see if you can guess the kinds of punctuation and print type that I used in my writing.

- Model with a piece of teacher-written text.

Turn and talk to the person next to you. What punctuation marks and print type do you think I used in this page of the story based on how my voice changed as I read the words?

- Chart student responses.
- Show them the writing to see the actual punctuation.

Independent Practice

- Give each pair a piece of writing at their own level or a page in a book to practice reading with intonation and fluency.
- Distribute the Fluency Unit Assessment (Resource 5.2).

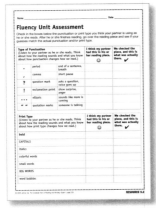

Listen carefully to your partner as he or she reads a page in a book. Your partner will not show you the punctuation or print type until afterwards, so while he or she is reading, write down on your assessment sheet what punctuation or print type you think he or she is reading and why you think that. Remember to take turns and use all we have learned about how our voice changes to match these conventions!

Wrap-Up

Over the last two weeks we have learned all about reading like we talk. We have learned that using punctuation, print type, and phrases changes how we read and helps us to sound better as readers and understand what we are reading. Remember to keep practicing this as you read from now on!

Using Fluency and Phrasing to Enhance Our Writing

Why Teach This?

- To show students the connection between reading and writing conventions.
- To teach students how punctuation and print type can change the emphasis in a piece of writing.
- To teach students the importance of conventions in writing.

Framing Question

- How do writers use punctuation and print type to make their writing sound better and to emphasize certain parts?

Unit Goals

- Students will learn to use proper punctuation at the ends of sentences.
- Students will begin to use punctuation to show emphasis.
- Students will begin to use print type to show emphasis.
- Students will understand how punctuation and print type change the meaning in their writing.

Anchor Texts

- *Bark, George* by Jules Feiffer
- *Don't Let Pigeon Drive the Bus!* by Mo Willems
- *Move Over!* by Joy Cowley
- *The Night I Followed the Dog* by Nina Laden
- *Yo! Yes?* by Chris Raschka

Resource Sheets

- Fluency and Conventions Writing Homework (Resource 5.3)
- Print Type Homework (Resource 5.4)
- Peer Editing Sheet (Resource 5.5)
- Using Fluency and Phrasing Unit Reflection (Resource 5.6)
- Writing Celebration Comments Sheet (Resource 5.7)

Unit Assessment Using Fluency and Phrasing to Enhance Our Writing			CONVENTIONS
Student name:	EMERGING	DEVELOPING	INDEPENDENT
Identifies varied punctuation marks.			
Uses correct punctuation at the ends of sentences.			
Understands how punctuation changes the emphasis in our writing.			
Identifies varied print type.			
Uses print type to emphasize something.			
Understands how print type changes the emphasis in our writing.			
Uses punctuation and print type purposefully and with intention.			

Stage of the Unit	Focused Instruction You will	Independent Practice Students will
IMMERSION 1 day	• read *Yo! Yes?* and do a punctuation search as you read, looking for various punctuation marks in the book.	• work with a partner to do a punctuation search in favorite read-aloud books, marking punctuation marks with sticky notes.
IDENTIFICATION 1 day	• read from *Wolf!* and model how periods and commas help readers read with fluency. • using student writing, model places to fill in punctuation or varied print type.	• look through a piece of writing from the beginning of the year to try and find some places to add punctuation and/or print type.

GUIDED PRACTICE
8 days
	• using your own writing, model how periods and commas can change writing.
	• model how question marks can change writing.
	• model how exclamation points can change writing; read *I Lost My Bear*.
	• model how ellipses can change writing; read *Bark, George*.
	• model how bold letters, italics, and big and small words can change writing; read *Don't Let Pigeon Drive the Bus!*
	• model how to peer edit.
		• work with a piece of writing from earlier in the year to practice the following:
		  • adding a period at the end of a sentence
		  • adding a comma to pause
		  • adding an exclamation point to show excitement or anger
		  • adding an ellipsis to show that more is coming
		  • adding quotation marks when someone is speaking
		  • adding print type to make the writing sound and look more interesting
		  • using punctuation and print type in writing with intention
		• practice editing the writing with their partner.

COMMITMENT 1 day	• reflect on how your writing has changed using these conventions.	• celebrate a piece of writing with a small group where they used punctuation and print type with intention.
TOTAL: 11 DAYS		

Getting Started

In this unit students will go back to a piece of writing from earlier in the school year. They will quickly use what was learned during the reading unit to change their writing, adding punctuation and print type. Students are very enthusiastic about this unit.

Teaching Materials

For this writing unit, use many of the books listed for the reading unit. Use these books to show students ways to use punctuation and print type while conferencing with them and helping them to envision these elements in their own writing. Students' writing and teacher-created writing can also be used as models.

Stages of the Unit

Immersion

One of the benefits of following the reading unit with this writing unit on conventions is that students have already been immersed in punctuation and print type. We recommend starting this writing unit about one week into the reading unit, so the information they are learning in reading is fresh in the writer's mind. The unit begins with a brief review of punctuation marks, as students search for them in favorite books. Send home a parent letter at this time to encourage families to support your work.

Identification

During the Identification stage we will transfer students' knowledge of punctuation and print type into their writing. Students go back to an older piece of writing from their folders and highlight the punctuation and or print type they used. Ask them to think about what they have noticed about this work.

Guided Practice

During Guided Practice, students will look at their writing from a reader's point of view. Is the punctuation supportive of what they are trying to convey? Is it easy to navigate through the text? Students are asked to slow down and reread work to check for necessary punctuation. They are asked to spend some time editing for conventions and print type.

Commitment

Students publish or re-publish (if they used an old piece of writing) one piece of writing that shows evidence of their knowledge of print type and punctuation. The class will spend time sharing new writing that conveys a message with more emphasis and enthusiasm.

Dear Parents,

We are following our Sounding Like Readers unit with a writing unit on Fluency and Conventions. We have learned that punctuation and print type (capital letters, italics, small print, and colorful print) are very important for showing emphasis when we read. Now we are using this knowledge to think about how to show emphasis in our own writing. Students will be doing the following:

- learning to use proper punctuation at the ends of sentences in their writing
- beginning to use punctuation to show emphasis in their writing
- beginning to use print type to show emphasis in their writing
- understanding how punctuation and print type change the meaning in their own writing

In order to support our work, please emphasize the use of punctuation and print type when your child is writing. Our proper use of punctuation directly relates to the meaning of the print we write. Help your child use punctuation and print type to convey meaning and emphasis in his or her writing.

Warmly,

Above is a letter you can send to parents to help support their children's learning in this unit.

Day-by-Day Lessons

DAY 1 Immersion

Focused Instruction

Today we're going to start a new unit on punctuation and print type. Before we start looking at our own writing, we're going to do a punctuation search in a book we already know. When we do our search, we're going to look for the punctuation marks the author uses and think about why he chose to use them.

- Read *Yo! Yes?* Stop during the reading at specific punctuation marks to notice them and think about why they might have been used.

Independent Practice

Today you're going to work with a partner to go through some favorite read-aloud books. Each partnership will get three sticky notes to mark punctuation they find in their books. Try to mark three different kinds of punctuation marks and see if you can find some unusual ones.

Wrap-Up

All of you used your sticky notes to mark punctuation in your books. I'm going to ask two pairs of students to share their finds with the class.

DAY 2 Identification

Focused Instruction

We have spent some of our reading time thinking and learning about punctuation and print type. We have learned that this changes how we read, affects our fluency, and deepens our comprehension. Now we are going to think and learn how to use this same punctuation and print type in our writing. We use punctuation in our writing to tell the reader when to slow down, stop, or pause. We use punctuation in our writing to tell the reader when we are asking a question, when more is coming, or when to feel certain emotions. We do this by putting punctuation and print type into our own writing just like the authors of our favorite read-alouds do.

Independent Practice

Take out your writing folders and look through a piece of your writing from the beginning or middle of the year. Spend some time looking for punctuation or print type. You may find that you do not have very much, if any. If this is the case, try to find a piece of writing that has even a little punctuation. Think about what punctuation you have used and how it supports the writing. Put a sticky note on the page where you noticed the most punctuation or print type. Name the punctuation and print type by writing it on the sticky note.

- Some children have used punctuation in their past writing, and some may only have periods and not a lot of variety. The purpose of this unit is to help children use punctuation and print type with intention.

Wrap-Up

Many of you found some punctuation and print type in your writing. Let's chart the kinds of punctuation we have used so we can think about other types of punctuation we may want to add. Post the sticky notes on the chart.

- Here is an example of a chart to support this work. This chart can be used throughout the study.

> Put your sticky notes under the punctuation marks you used in your writing.
>
> | . | ? | , | ! | ... |

We have found punctuation in our reading and in our writing. Punctuation changes the way we read and makes stories easier to understand and sound better.

DAY 3 Guided Practice

Focused Instruction

Let's think about periods and commas. A period comes at the end of a sentence. A comma is used to show a slight pause or to separate things in a list. We need periods at the end of a sentence in order for the writing to make sense. If we do not have them, your voice does not know when to stop or pause and everything gets mushed together. Let's look at the book Wolf! *Did you notice when Wolf went to read to the animals and he forgot to take a breath, all the words were mushed together and you could not understand him?*

- Create a chart like the one below on Days 2 through 5, adding at least one definition each day.

Ways We Can Use Punctuation in Our Writing
A <u>period</u> (**.**) is used at the end of a sentence.
<u>Commas</u> (**,**) are used to show a slight pause in a sentence or to separate words in a list.
A <u>question mark</u> (**?**) is placed at the end of sentence or phrase that is a direct question.
An <u>exclamation point</u> (**!**) is used to show excitement, eagerness, nervousness, or to emphasize something.
An <u>ellipsis</u> (**...**) is used to show that there is more coming.
<u>Quotation marks</u> (**" "**) are used to show that someone is talking.

Independent Practice

Your writing work today is to go back to an old piece of writing and make sure you have periods at the end of your sentences. If you find a place where a comma belongs instead, you can add that, too. If you finish working on one piece of older writing, look for another to work on.

- This is a good time to have one-on-one conferences to clear up any confusions about how to use specific punctuation.

Wrap-Up

Turn to the person next to you and share a place where you used punctuation.

DAY 4 Guided Practice

Focused Instruction

A question mark is used when someone in a story is asking a question. We learned that when we see a question mark our voice goes up. Writers also use a question mark when there is a question in their book. Turn to the person next to you and ask them a question, practicing making your voice go up as you ask.

Independent Practice

Your writing work today is to reread an old piece of writing or look at the piece you are now working on to see if there are places where you need a question mark. If there are no places to put a question mark, just continue to work on your writing and be aware of putting in punctuation where needed.

Wrap-Up

A few of you found places to add a question mark where there was a question in your writing. How did this change the sound of what you've written?

DAY 5 Guided Practice

Focused Instruction

Writers use an exclamation point to show excitement, anger, frustration, happiness, or other big emotions. We use an exclamation point to make something stand out in our writing. Let's look again at I Lost My Bear. *In this book you see a lot of exclamation points. Turn to the person next to you and talk about why there are so many exclamation points in this book.*

- Chart the responses.

Independent Practice

Take out the writing you are working on and find a place where you could use an exclamation point to show excitement, anger, frustration, happiness, or another strong emotion.

Wrap-Up

Turn to the person next to you and show him or her a place where you used an exclamation point. Practice reading that part the way it now sounds with the exclamation point.

DAY 6 Guided Practice

Focused Instruction

Writers use an ellipsis to show that more is coming and to raise excitement. Let's look again at Bark, George *at the places where an ellipsis is used before you find out what animal the doctor is going to pull out of George. Hannah and Thomas have also used ellipses in their writing to show that more is coming and to build your excitement.*

Independent Practice

Your writing work today is to find a place in your writing where you can add an ellipsis. Remember, an ellipsis means that more is coming and something big or exciting might happen.

- Students will continue to work on either a new piece of writing or going back to an old piece to try using an ellipsis.
- Use anchor texts such as *Bark, George* to confer with students, modeling the use of punctuation.

Wrap-Up

- Share examples from students who tried using ellipses in their writing.

DAY 7 Guided Practice

Focused Instruction

The last type of punctuation on our chart is quotation or talking marks. We use quotation marks to show that someone is talking. They often come before the word said or a word that means said, like exclaimed, yelled, screamed, and others. Not all books use quotation marks, and some writers use them more than others. Here is an example of a place where I could use quotation marks in this story I wrote about baking cookies with my friend.

- Model, using teacher writing or a child's writing, a good place to use quotation marks.

Independent Practice

Your writing work today is to see if there is a place where you think quotation or talking marks could go. You may not find a place, and that is okay, but then remember to check for the other punctuation we have learned as well.

- Quotation marks may confuse first graders, but it is important to introduce the concept. The goal is exposure, so children know what the marks are called and become familiar with them but cannot necessarily use them correctly yet in their writing.

Wrap-Up

- Choose a piece of student writing in which quotation marks have been added and share with the class.
- Send Fluency and Conventions Writing Homework (Resource 5.3) home with students.

DAY 8 Guided Practice

Focused Instruction

Now that we have looked at our writing and added punctuation, we can go back and look for places to add print type to make the writing more interesting for our readers. We can add print type to our words and to our pictures. We can put bold print and capital letters inside word bubbles to show someone is talking. Or we can use small and big words to emphasize parts of our writing. Remember the book Don't Let Pigeon Drive the Bus!? *The author uses a lot of different print types to change the meaning and how we read.*

• Create a chart like the one below and share it with students on Days 8 and 9.

Print type changes the way we read.
BOLD
CAPITALS
Italics
Colorful letters
small and BIG words
word bubbles

Independent Practice

Your writing work today is to choose one piece of writing that you have carefully worked on with punctuation. Use that same piece of writing and add some print type to either the pictures or the words.

Wrap-Up

Students who met in conferences share how they used different print type in their writing to emphasize certain things.

• Send Print Type Homework (Resource 5.4) home with students.

DAY 9 Guided Practice

Focused Instruction

One of the best ways to see whether we have put punctuation and/or print type in the right places is to look at a friend's work and read it for them. This is called peer editing. It is sometimes hard to see where we need to make changes in our own work, but it is easier to see where to make changes in a friend's writing. This is something I do with my friends after I write. I ask them to read it for me to see if there are any places where I can make some changes that make sense. You do not always have to agree to the changes, but it can help you to find some things that you may have missed on your own.

Independent Practice

• Distribute Peer Editing (Resource 5.5).

Your writing work today is to work with your friend and help to peer edit for punctuation and print type. Use the peer editing sheet to check for the things that you need. It is okay if you do not finish today; we will have time to look at the writing again tomorrow.

Wrap-Up

All of you worked very well with your partners today. One really good way of getting help with your writing is to have someone read it with you.

DAY 10 Guided Practice

Focused Instruction

Today we will continue to work with our partners to peer edit. Good partners take turns and are respectful of each other's work. Remember, you are working together to help each other find places where you used or can use punctuation and/or print type to make your writing better.

Independent Practice

Your writing work is to continue to peer edit with your partner. Remember, you are looking for punctuation and print type used correctly to make the writing more interesting for the reader.

Wrap-Up

Reflect on peer editing. How did it go for you? What was fun about it? What was hard about it? Talk to the partners next to you about how editing went today.

DAY 11 Commitment

Focused Instruction

We have spent the past two weeks learning how to use punctuation and print type to make our writing better. We are ready to reflect on the work we did using a reflection sheet. Then we will celebrate our writing with some friends.

- Put students in small sharing groups, preferably from another table so they can hear different writing.

Independent Practice

- Distribute Using Fluency and Phrasing Unit Reflection (Resource 5.6) and the Writing Celebration Comments (Resource 5.7).

Your writing work is to respond to the questions on the reflection sheet and then meet with your sharing groups to celebrate the hard work you have done using punctuation and print type to make your stories even better. Write a comment to a friend on the comment page.

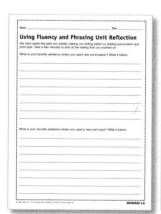

Wrap-Up

We have learned a lot in this unit about how to use punctuation and print type to make our writing sound better and give more meaning to the reader.

Strengthening Talk, Strengthening Bonds

First graders are deeply social beings. They are just learning how to engage with one another in a variety of ways. Explicit lessons on how to partner will fortify them for the next units. In reading time, the partner unit is one on stamina. As the year begins to draw to a close, we want to leave our students with strong messages about how to build their reading muscles, and to continue to do so through the summer. This small unit shares with our students the best tips for how to read long and strong.

Building Stamina: Reading Long and Strong   PROCESS

Why Teach This?

- To strengthen students' reading stamina so they can read for a longer period of time.
- To strengthen students' reading comprehension.
- To teach students that reading can happen in many different places and under many different conditions.

Framing Questions

- How do you increase reading stamina?
- How does reading stamina increase comprehension?

Unit Goals

- Students will learn to read for a longer period of time.
- Students will learn how reading longer can strengthen reading comprehension.
- Students will learn that reading can happen in many different places.

Anchor Texts

- *Animal Homes* by Bobbi Kalman
- *Biscuit* by Alyssa Capucilli
- "Dreams" by Langston Hughes (*The Collected Poems of Langston Hughes*)
- *Henry and Mudge and the Wild Wind* by Cynthia Rylant
- *The Legend of Mexicatl* by Jo Harper
- *Reading Makes You Feel Good* by Todd Parr

Unit Assessment Building Stamina: Reading Long and Strong			PROCESS
Student name:	EMERGING	DEVELOPING	INDEPENDENT
Reads for a longer period of time than before starting the unit.			
Understands how reading longer can help with comprehension.			
Chooses longer books that still feel level.			
Understands rereading for meaning and for enjoyment.			

Stage of the Unit	Focused Instruction You will	Independent Practice Students will
IMMERSION 2 days	• visit a second-grade classroom during independent reading and notice how the students read "long and strong." • reflect on how you feel when you are reading strong.	• talk to a partner about what they notice the second-grade readers doing during independent reading that may look different from what first graders do. • think about themselves as readers during independent time, and what they need to feel like so they can read long and strong.
IDENTIFICATION 1 day	• chart with students ways to read longer and stronger. • identify what makes it easier to read for a longer period of time.	• talk to a partner about ways that they feel they can read longer and stronger during independent reading.
GUIDED PRACTICE 7 days	• demonstrate reading longer and stronger by taking a picture walk using the book *Henry and Mudge and the Wild Wind.* • demonstrate reading longer and stronger by rereading a book you love, like *Reading Makes You Feel Good.* • demonstrate reading longer and stronger by choosing interesting books such as *Animal Homes* or *The Legend of Mexicatl.* • demonstrate reading longer and stronger by choosing different genres (pick one fiction book, one nonfiction book, and one poetry book). • demonstrate reading longer and stronger by reading mostly level books. • demonstrate reading longer and stronger by reading from the Biscuit series so you can go on to the next book. • demonstrate reading longer and stronger by reading until the bell on the timer rings. • chart the different places where readers read.	• practice reading stronger and longer by taking a picture walk. • practice reading longer and stronger by rereading a book they love. • practice reading longer and stronger by choosing very interesting books. • practice reading longer and stronger by choosing different genres. • practice reading longer and stronger by having mostly level books. • practice reading longer and stronger by reading from a series so they can go on to the next book when they finish. • practice reading longer and stronger by reading until the bell on the timer rings.
COMMITMENT 1 day	• reflect on your reading stamina and how your book choices made your reading stronger.	• reflect on and celebrate with a partner some of the books that helped them to read longer and stronger.
TOTAL: 11 DAYS		

Becoming Strong Partners: Supporting Each Other as Writers

PROCESS

Why Teach This?

- To teach students how writers collaborate throughout the writing process to improve their writing.
- To build a writing community that is supportive and cooperative.

Framing Questions

- How do writers work together to improve their writing?
- What are writing partners?

Unit Goals

- Students will generate writing ideas with a partner.
- Students will tell stories from their lives with a partner.
- Students will check in with a partner during writing to support each other.
- Students will work cooperatively to figure out hard words.
- Students will share their writing with a partner and respond positively to each other's work.

Anchor Text

- *Big Al* by Andrew Clements and Yoshi

Unit Assessment Becoming Strong Partners: Supporting Each Other as Writers PROCESS			
Student name:	**EMERGING**	**DEVELOPING**	**INDEPENDENT**
Generates writing ideas with a partner.			
Tells stories from his or her life with a partner.			
Checks in with a partner during writing and gets right back to work when done.			
Works cooperatively to decode difficult words.			
Responds positively and authentically to a partner's work.			

Stage of the Unit	Focused Instruction You will	Independent Practice Students will
IMMERSION 2 days	• read *Big Al*; discuss how working together can be more powerful than being alone; model with another adult how writing partners work together to generate ideas, talking back and forth about what ideas they have for writing; ask students what they notice about how the partners work together.	• talk with a partner before writing to generate ideas and brainstorm writing topics, and then when they have an idea, write about it independently.

IMMERSION (continued)	• model with another adult how writing partners work together during writing by checking in to see how it is going, asking for spelling help, and also letting each other work silently; ask students what they notice about how the partners work together.	• sit with a partner during writing time to support each other.
IDENTIFICATION 1 day	• start class chart, How Do Writing Partners Help Each Other? and chart student responses based on their observations on Days 1 and 2.	• work with a partner to generate ideas before writing and to support each other during writing.
GUIDED PRACTICE 6 days	• model how writing partners generate ideas, emphasizing that partners take turns talking and listening. • model how writers tell stories from their lives that they might want to write about, stories that are funny or interesting. • discuss how writing partners check in with each other during writing; model what this looks like and how writers get right back to work quickly. • model how writers can practice spelling strategies together when they get stuck on a word; emphasize that if they can't figure it out exactly, they do the best they can and then get back to writing. • model how writers share their work with each other at the end of writing and listen without interrupting while their partner reads his or her work; demonstrate positive feedback that writers can give to their partners.	• work with a partner to generate writing ideas, making sure that they are taking turns. • share stories from their lives with a partner, deciding if any of the stories might make a good writing project. • practice checking in with their writing partner during reading. • work with their partners during Independent Practice to figure out hard words together, if needed. • write with their partner, each working on their own piece individually; at the end of writing time, share their writing piece and respond positively to their partner's writing.
COMMITMENT 1 day	• draw a picture of two writers working together cooperatively.	• draw a picture of their writing partnership working together cooperatively (children getting along, taking turns, etc.); hang student pictures in the writing center/area.
TOTAL: 10 DAYS		

The Lovely Rhythms of Language

Summer is peeking in the windows, and poetry is blooming. Your first graders will savor the sound of language: they love to sing and to feel the rhythms of the world. This month should feel raucous and tender, joyful and serene, funny and serious, all at once. Just like your first graders, a seeming contradiction in terms, poetry is both structure and freedom. And that is what first grade is all about.

Exploring the Sound of Poetry

GENRE

Why Teach This?
- To expose students to the genre of poetry.
- To teach students the various strategies readers use when reading poems.
- To teach students how readers interpret poems using their own experiences and emotions.

Framing Questions
- How do readers read poetry?
- How do readers think about poems?

Unit Goals
- Students will identify qualities of poetry.
- Students will examine white space on the page and discuss how it may connect to the poem.
- Students will identify shape poems.
- Students will identify rhyming and nonrhyming poems.
- Students will visualize while reading poems.
- Students will consider how a poem makes them feel.
- Students will summarize a poem in one or two sentences.

Anchor Texts
- "April Rain Song" and "Poem," by Langston Hughes (*The Collected Poems of Langston Hughes*)
- "Chairs" by Valerie Worth (*All the Small Poems and Fourteen More*)
- "Moon, Have You Seen My Mother?" by Karla Kuskin
- *Off the Sweet Shores of Africa and Other Talking Drum Rhymes* by Uzo Unobagha
- "Sick" by Shel Silverstein (*Where the Sidewalk Ends*)
- "Sliding Board" by Kay Winters (*Did You See What I Saw? Poems About School*)

Unit Assessment Exploring the Sound of Poetry			GENRE
Student name:	EMERGING	DEVELOPING	INDEPENDENT
Distinguishes poetry from fiction and nonfiction.			
Examines white space on the page and discusses how it may connect to a poem.			
Identifies shape poems.			
Identifies rhyming and nonrhyming poems.			
Visualizes while reading a poem.			
Summarizes a poem into one or two sentences.			

Stage of the Unit	Focused Instruction You will	Independent Practice Students will
IMMERSION 1 day	• ask students what they know about poetry. • discuss where students have read or seen poetry before and how they define it; share a couple of your favorite poems with the class.	• choose from a variety of leveled poems, reading a few during Independent Practice. • share one thing they noticed while reading a poem with a partner.
IDENTIFICATION 1 day	• point out that most poetry is shorter than fiction or nonfiction; ask students what they notice by looking at and listening to different poems.	• jot one thing they notice that makes poetry different from fiction or nonfiction books.
GUIDED PRACTICE 11 days	• read "Moon, Have You Seen My Mother?"; think aloud about what you see when you look at the poem; discuss the idea of "white space" on the page and how it affects how you read the poem. • read "Chairs" by Valerie Worth; think aloud about what you see when you look at the poem; identify the shape of the poem and explain that some poems are written in shapes.	• identify how poets use white space in the poems they read; identify one poem that experiments with white space and share it with a partner. • look for shapes in the poems they read during Independent Practice. • see if they can find rhyming words in the poems they read independently. • identify poems they read that do not rhyme and think about what words the poet uses to make them poetic or beautiful.

GUIDED PRACTICE (continued)	• read "Sick" by Shel Silverstein; ask students to listen for what they hear when the poem is read; discuss how some poems rhyme and ask students to identify rhyming words they hear. • read "Sliding Board" and practice reading it aloud together, having fun with the sounds of the poem. • read "April Rain Song" by Langston Hughes; model reading it once, then stopping during a second reading to close your eyes and make pictures of what you hear. • read a poem from *Off the Sweet Shore of Africa* and appreciate the sound of the words. • reread "Poem" by Langston Hughes; model how readers use what they remember or know to help imagine a poem in their minds; describe a time when you felt the same feelings the poem is conveying. • reread "April Rain Song" by Langston Hughes and model summarizing the poem in only one or two sentences; describe that sometimes readers want to tell someone what a poem is mostly about quickly.	• stop while reading poems to make pictures in their minds of what they read. • think about their feelings when reading poems. • pick one poem they read during independent reading to read aloud and listen for special beats. • use what they remember or know to help imagine a poem in their minds (and draw an image of it). • meet with a partner to read a poem and enjoy the sound of it together. • choose one poem during Independent Practice that they will read aloud with a partner. • choose a poem to share with a partner and either act out, sing, or dramatize it in some way.
COMMITMENT 2 days	• choose a favorite poem that you want to share with the class; demonstrate how readers read poetry aloud, taking time to savor each word and using a clear, loud voice so listeners can hear. • read aloud your favorite poem for the class.	• choose a favorite poem they want to share with the class; practice reading it aloud, taking time to savor each word and reading in a loud, clear voice. • read aloud their favorite poem for the class.
TOTAL: 15 DAYS		

Becoming Poets: Words That Sing

Why Teach This?

- To expose students to the genre of poetry.
- To teach students the difference between poetry and stories.
- To give students the opportunity to write a variety of poems.

Framing Questions

- What is poetry?
- How are poems different from stories in the way they sound and look?
- How do poets write poems?

Unit Goals

- Students will recognize the look and sound of a poem.
- Students will distinguish a poem from a story.
- Students will write a list poem.
- Students will write a poem using sensory images.
- Students will experiment with white space in their poems.
- Students will attempt repetition in a short poem.
- Students will revise and rework a poem in preparation for a poetry café.

Anchor Texts

- "Her Daddy's Hands" by Angela Johnson (*In Daddy's Arms I Am Tall*)
- "One Inch Tall" by Shel Silverstein (*Where the Sidewalk Ends*)
- "Ready for Sleep" and "If You're Tired and You Know It" by Bruce Lansky (*Sweet Dreams: Bedtime Poems, Songs, and Lullabies*)
- "What I'd Cook for My Teacher" by Bruce Lansky (*If Pigs Could Fly*)

Unit Assessment Becoming Poets: Words That Sing			GENRE
Student name:	EMERGING	DEVELOPING	INDEPENDENT
Recognizes the look of a poem.			
Distinguishes a poem from a story.			
Writes a list poem.			
Writes a short poem using sensory images.			
Experiments with white space in their poems.			
Uses repetition in a short poem.			
Rewrites the title of a poem to convey a message to the reader.			
Revises a poem by examining word choice.			

Stage of the Unit	Focused Instruction You will	Independent Practice Students will
IMMERSION 4 days	• read one or two poems several times; ask students how poems sound different from stories. • identify how poems are different from stories and make a chart listing these differences. • read "If You're Tired and You Know It" aloud and discuss how it feels when reading; try reading it several different ways; try it accompanied by music or clapping.	• write whatever they consider to be a poem. • read poems aloud to themselves or a friend; play with different ways to read the poems aloud. • practice reading poems aloud with accompanying music.
IDENTIFICATION 1 day	• start class chart, What Do Poets Do?, and use it to name techniques and show an example of each; read "What I'd Cook for My Teacher" and introduce list poems; write one as a class.	• write list poems on special paper.
GUIDED PRACTICE 12 days	• model how poets get ideas for list poems; write a new list poem as a class. • share a sensory poem "Ready for Sleep." • model how poets choose different kinds of papers for the poems they want to write; write either a list or sensory poem on different kinds of paper. • demonstrate using one or two senses to write a poem, thinking aloud during writing; ask students to pick what sense they would like to focus on during writing for the day. • read "One Inch Tall" and model how poets use their imagination to invent what they want to write about and then write what is in their heads.	• brainstorm a new idea for a list poem and write one on poetry paper (paper with no lines, or paper with lines in different places all over the page). • choose a poetry paper that fits the poem they want to write. • write sensory poems using one or two senses on poetry paper. • imagine something they want to write about and share with a writing buddy before writing poems for the day. • experiment with white space on the paper while writing poems. • write poems using repetition, choosing which paper they want to use.

GUIDED PRACTICE *(continued)*	• discuss how poets use white space; write a poem, thinking aloud about white space and the position of words on the page. • introduce repetition as a poetry technique; reread "If You're Tired and You Know It." • write a poem that uses repetition as a class. • examine how poets choose titles for their poems that convey a message to the reader; revisit poems you have read aloud and examine the titles of each. • model how you can sing or chant or dramatize a poem you wrote.	• revisit poems to look at their titles; choose one title they love to share with a partner. • revisit one of their poems and rewrite the title to convey a message to the reader. • share a poem they love with a partner and sing or dramatize it. • share a poem they wrote with a partner and sing it or dramatize it.
COMMITMENT 3 days	• demonstrate the process of choosing one poem to revise and publish. • model how poets revise a poem by looking at word choice. • demonstrate how poets read their work at a "poetry café."	• reread the poems they have written and choose one poem they want to revise and publish. • read the poem they chose and look carefully at the words they used; change the words in their poems to make them more rhythmic, where possible. • share their work in a class "poetry café."
TOTAL: 20 DAYS		

Precious Days Past and Future

Summer is around the corner. Your young ones are dreaming of long summer days. You too are thinking ahead, planning a beach read or making plans for summer work. While our minds naturally wander in those directions, let us engage in units that celebrate the forward-thinking mind and help our children make plans for the summer that will include reading and writing. It is far too long a time to be without attention to words, and without work on print. If we can speak to our students about our expectations and bring joy to that work, they will be far more likely to pursue a summer of independent reading and writing. And the benefits are enormous. Armed with a special summer writing notebook and a plan for books they will read and borrow (maybe your school can provide each child with a bag or box of books for summer reading—a great grant request!), they leave your rooms full of the gifts you have given them: the love of language and a confidence with text. These gifts will be endless, always useful, and never forgotten. So, too, are their gifts to us.

Looking Back, Looking Forward: Making Summer Reading Plans

PROCESS

Why Teach This?
- To reflect on the reading work done over the school year.
- To make plans for summer reading.

Framing Questions
- How did your reading grow and change during this school year?
- What are some reading goals you have for the summer?

Unit Goals
- Students will reflect on themselves as readers: favorite books, favorite reading spots, strategies learned, favorite genres, struggles, and successes.
- Students will make plans for summer reading.

Anchor Texts
- *Abuela* by Arthur Dorros
- *The Friendly Four* by Eloise Greenfield
- *What You Know First* by Patricia MacLachlan

Unit Assessment Looking Back, Looking Forward: Making Summer Reading Plans			PROCESS
Student name:	EMERGING	DEVELOPING	INDEPENDENT
Identifies qualities in self as a reader.			
Identifies some favorite books, authors, and/or genres.			
Identifies what has changed in reading life since the beginning of first grade.			
Makes plans for summer reading.			

Looking Back

Stage of the Unit	Focused Instruction You will	Independent Practice Students will
IMMERSION 1 day	• reflect on our year as readers. • model thinking aloud about some of your favorite read-alouds and favorite reading units and activities.	• work with a partner and talk about at least one favorite read-aloud and why it's a favorite. • work with a partner and reflect on a favorite reading unit and/or reading activity and why they liked it.
IDENTIFICATION 1 day	• name and identify ways we can reflect on ourselves as readers: favorite books, favorite genres, favorite activity, what we can now do as readers, reading successes, and reading struggles.	• identify a time in first grade when reading felt like a struggle and a time when they felt really strong readers; share with a partner.
GUIDED PRACTICE 5 days	• read *Abuela* (or another favorite read-aloud); discuss why it is a favorite. • reflect on a reading activity from the year and discuss why it meant something to you. • discuss one of your favorite genres and why. • discuss a time when reading felt tricky this year and why. • discuss a time when you felt strong as a reader.	• pick a favorite read-aloud and share it with a partner. • make a list of their favorite books from the year and share with a partner; discuss genres studied (fiction, nonfiction, letters, signs, and poetry) and discuss which ones they enjoyed the most. • reflect on strategies they now have for dealing with tricky spots and write them on a list. • reflect on a time when they felt strong as readers and discuss this with a partner.
COMMITMENT 1 day	• reflect on your favorite books and make a pile of them to start with as read-alouds next year.	• celebrate themselves as readers, sharing their book lists, observations, and reflections with a small group.
TOTAL: 8 DAYS		

Looking Forward

Stage of the Unit	Focused Instruction You will	Independent Practice Students will
IMMERSION 1 day	• read *The Friendly Four*; discuss summer plans; discuss places where you can read over the summer. • discuss the kinds of books you plan to read over the summer.	• work with a partner and make a list of the places where they can read and the kinds of books they will choose to read over the summer.
IDENTIFICATION 1 day	• determine what things you will want in your summer reading box; chart with the class.	• decorate their summer reading boxes in ways that will motivate and excite them as readers.
GUIDED PRACTICE 5 days	• model setting reading goals for the summer, including books you will read and where you will read them. • model getting book recommendations from a friend (have another teacher come in and recommend a book to you). • model using sticky notes to reflect as a reader. • model keeping notes in a reading journal, either pictures of a favorite part or writing about a book. • read aloud *What You Know First* and talk about the books that started our year.	• write a reading goal for the summer. • draw a picture of places where they can see themselves reading over the summer. • write book recommendations on index cards for friends to put into their summer reading boxes. • talk with a partner about some ways that they can use sticky notes as readers this summer. • decorate their summer reading journals. • make a list of books or types of books they hope to read over the summer.
COMMITMENT 1 day	• celebrate summer reading boxes, listing what is now in them.	• celebrate their summer reading boxes with a partner.
TOTAL: 8 DAYS		

Looking Back, Looking Forward: Making Summer Writing Plans

Why Teach This?

- To reflect on the writing work done over the school year.
- To make plans for summer writing.

Framing Questions

- How did your writing grow and change during this school year?
- What are some writing goals you have for the summer?

Unit Goals

- Students will reflect on themselves as writers: favorite books they wrote, favorite writing study, struggles, and successes.
- Students will make plans for summer writing.

Anchor Texts

- *The Friendly Four* by Eloise Greenfield
- *The Night Before Summer Vacation* by Natasha Wing and Julie Durrell
- *The Pattaconk Brook* by James Stevenson

Unit Assessment Looking Back, Looking Forward: Making Summer Writing Plans			PROCESS
Student name:	**EMERGING**	**DEVELOPING**	**INDEPENDENT**
Identifies qualities of self as a writer.			
Reflects on self as a writer: what has changed in his or her writing life since the beginning of first grade.			
Makes plans for summer writing.			

Looking Back

Stage of the Unit	Focused Instruction You will	Independent Practice Students will
IMMERSION 1 day	• revisit the word *reflection* and explain how we are going to think back on our year as writers. • model thinking aloud about some of your writing pieces from the school year.	• work with a partner and talk about at least one favorite published book. • work with a partner and reflect on a favorite writing unit or writing activity and why it was a favorite.
IDENTIFICATION 1 day	• name and identify ways we can reflect on ourselves as writers: favorite books you have written, favorite genres, favorite writing activity, what you can now do as a writer, writing successes, and writing struggles.	• identify a time in first grade when writing felt like a struggle and another time when writing flowed easily; share with a partner.
GUIDED PRACTICE 5 days	• model rereading a favorite writing piece. • reflect on a writing activity from the year and discuss why it meant something to you. • discuss one of your favorite writing genres and why. • reflect on times writing felt hard. • discuss a time when you felt strong as a writer.	• pick a favorite published piece and share it with a partner. • discuss favorite writing topics. • discuss genres studied (fiction, nonfiction, letters, signs, and poetry) and talk about which ones were their favorite to write. • reflect on strategies they now have when they get stuck as a writer and make a list of these. • reflect on a time when they felt strong as a writer and discuss this with a partner.
COMMITMENT 1 day	• reflect on your favorite writing activity. • make a commitment to write over the summer.	• celebrate themselves as writers and share their books with a small group. • make a commitment to write over the summer.
TOTAL: 8 DAYS		

Looking Forward

Stage of the Unit	Focused Instruction You will	Independent Practice Students will
IMMERSION 1 day	• read *The Pattaconk Brook*; talk about how writers work hard to express themselves and how words are companions on the journey. • discuss the kinds of books you will write over the summer.	• make a short list of the places where they want to write this summer. • work with a partner and make a list of the places where they can write and the kinds of books they will write over the summer.
IDENTIFICATION 1 day	• determine what genres you may try to write in over the summer.	• decorate their summer writing notebooks.
GUIDED PRACTICE 5 days	• read *The Night Before Summer Vacation*; discuss how writers also have to get ready for their writing; model setting writing goals for the summer. • reflect on places you can write over the summer. • model writing in a journal. • revisit *The Friendly Four*; discuss how writing can record memories of our lives; model using writing as a way to remember special summer times. • model how to write letters to keep in touch with students and friends.	• write a writing goal for the summer. • draw a picture of places where they can see themselves writing over the summer. • decorate their summer writing journal. • make a list of ways they will try writing over the summer. • write the first page of their summer journal.
COMMITMENT 1 day	• celebrate and share a way you will write over the summer.	• celebrate their summer writing journals with a partner.
TOTAL: 8 DAYS		

Circular Seasons:
Endings and Beginnings

You will miss these children. And they will miss you. For the rest of their lives, they will remember your name. There should be more of a ritual for you to let go of these children and prepare to embrace the new ones.

In Japan every fall there is a traditional chrysanthemum festival to celebrate the last blooming before the winter comes. The people journey to view the beautiful flowers and to celebrate the changing seasons. There are special horticulturists who work for a full eleven months of the year to prepare for this festival, creating spectacular chrysanthemum arrangements, which they feature in *uwaya*, serene shelters for the beautiful plantings. In this way, people can contemplate and reflect upon the changing seasons.

I wish we had such a thing for the work we do. The seasons go by and then come around again. There is a beauty in that: we know they will always come again. But these, these precious children, they will never come again quite like this. Let these last days of the school year be an *uwaya* for us—a serene shelter for reflection. The work you do with your students is, well, once in a lifetime. Remember this as the seasons of your teaching life begin once again.

Chapter 6

TRACKING STUDENT PROGRESS ACROSS THE YEAR

The C4 Assessment

Assessment is the beginning, the middle, and the end of our teaching. It is the heart of our instruction, the age-old dilemma, the most gratifying, frustrating, and rewarding aspect of our work, because it reveals in stark relief: How are we all doing? Done well, it is not offensive, harmful, hurtful, or unpleasant for children. Done well, it is engaging, reflective, fascinating, and insightful for teachers. Done poorly, it is demeaning, demoralizing, and useless to everyone. Done poorly, it is unhelpful, uninteresting, and slightly boring. We have created rubrics as formative assessments and a yearlong assessment tool we call the C4 Assessment that we believe will lead you to the "done well" column. Done well, assessment is meaningful, as J. Richard Gentry (2008) points out: "...you can loop together assessment and instruction and use both simultaneously to support your students in targeted and powerful ways."

Unit Rubrics as Formative Assessments

Within each unit we have written for this book, we have given you a model assessment rubric such as the following:

Unit Assessment The ARCH: Building Independence: Reading Role Models			PROCESS
Student name:	EMERGING	DEVELOPING	INDEPENDENT
Follows routines of reading time.			
Makes book selections independently.			
Identifies personal reading goals.			
Works with a partner to share a book.			

These rubrics can and should be used as formative assessments. By this we mean that you can construct rubrics such as these with your students during the Identification stage of any unit. As you name the expectations for process behaviors, or the elements of a genre, or the type of strategy or convention you would like to see your students use, you can add this list of performance indicators to your rubric. Then you can give the rubric to your students to use during their Guided Practice. If we give students our upfront expectations in writing, and they have helped to form and understand these expectations, we can be sure that they will know what we want them to do as readers and writers. They can use these rubrics as placeholders for our teaching—reminding them on a daily basis what we want them to practice, even when we are not sitting next to them.

By keeping the rubric alongside your conferring conversations with individual readers and writers, you will be able to focus your observations and record your comments on how each student is performing throughout the length of the unit. Using the rubric to supplement your conferring plans will also allow you to refer back on these conversations to plan for future instruction—either for the entire class when you see something that nearly everyone is having difficulty with, or for individual or small-group work.

Unit Rubrics as Summative Assessments

Of course these rubrics can also be summative. You may use them to measure your students' performance at the end of each unit, and you may gather these collective unit assessments to plan and draft your report cards. We believe these rubrics will be extremely helpful on several levels. They will help you focus your instruction towards the expectations listed on the rubric. They will help guide and focus your students practice within any unit of study, and they will allow for self-reflection— for our students and for ourselves. By the end of any unit, we should be able to see what students accomplished, and what we still need to work on.

The C4 Assessment

Rubrics are not the only form of assessment that we would like you to consider. As our entire year has been built around the premise of balanced instruction across process, genre, strategy, and conventions, we would like to suggest that you consider your students' growing skills and abilities within these four categories. To help you accomplish this task, we have created the C4 Assessment (C4A) forms seen at the end of this chapter. These forms merge many of the teaching points across the year into collective assessments of students' understanding of process, genre, strategy, and conventions. The C4A is clear and simple to use, and yet provides a great deal of information for teachers, so that we may differentiate our instruction for all students; for parents so we may share students' growth or challenges; and for schools.

Tracking Our Students Across the Grades

We have designed specific C4 assessments for each grade level. While their format and organization are the same, the content varies as we have given a great deal of thought to the articulation of instruction across the grades. We recommend that these assessment forms be filled out each year and passed on to the next year's teacher. This will give teachers a clearer sense of their students as readers and writers at the beginning of the year than traditional packaged reading or writing assessments.

Using These Forms

There are many different ways to incorporate these forms into your year. You may choose to:

- use them to conduct a more formal review of student performance at the beginning, middle, and end of the year.
- keep these forms with your other conferring materials and use them to note when students demonstrate progress within a particular unit.
- keep these forms with you as you read through your students' published writing, so you can use their written work as evidence of learning.

No matter which method you use, we ask you to consider how your children are developing as readers and writers inside the Complete 4 components. What have they learned to do as readers and writers? What have they come to understand about genre? What have they learned about reading and writing strategies? What do they now understand about the world of conventions? Our job is to create lifelong readers and writers in our classrooms. Instruction-linked assessment through the Complete 4 is the key to achieving this objective.

Complete 4 Component: Process First Grade

KEY: **E**=emerging **D**=developing **I**=independent

Student: _____   School Year: _____

CAPACITIES:	BEGINNING OF THE YEAR	MIDDLE OF THE YEAR	END OF THE YEAR
Reads familiar text smoothly (fluency).			
Reads independently for 10 to 20 minutes (stamina).			
Selects books according to level and interest (independence).			
Explains personal criteria for choosing a book, poem, or story.			
Makes wise book choices according to purpose and interest (independence).			
Writes independently for 10 to 20 minutes (stamina).			
Uses prewriting tools to organize ideas and information (with support).			
Rereads own writing to add on to a picture, revise words, or fix spelling (independence).			
Attempts to spell new words with confidence (independence).			
Sustains a selected writing piece over two to five days (stamina).			
Sustains book talk independently for five to seven minutes (stamina).			
Reads at home independently or with others for seven minutes.			

ROLES:	BEGINNING OF THE YEAR	MIDDLE OF THE YEAR	END OF THE YEAR
Understands role while meeting in conference with a teacher.			
Is prepared for a conference with writing ready.			
Transitions from whole class to independent practice without assistance.			
Selects from various paper choices independently.			

Complete 4 Component: Process First Grade (continued)   KEY: **E**=emerging **D**=developing **I**=independent

Student: _____   School Year: _____

IDENTITIES:	BEGINNING OF THE YEAR	MIDDLE OF THE YEAR	END OF THE YEAR
Expresses ways that he or she has grown as a reader.			
Expresses ways that he or she has grown as a writer.			
Uses writing to communicate with others.			
Identifies various purposes for reading.			

COLLABORATION:	BEGINNING OF THE YEAR	MIDDLE OF THE YEAR	END OF THE YEAR
Sits knee to knee with a partner			
Looks at a book together with a partner.			
Articulates and shares reading experiences with others.			
Asks questions to clarify ideas and information.			
Responds during conversation by adding on to ideas.			
Interacts in positive, supportive ways with a partner.			

Complete 4 Component: Genre First Grade

KEY: **E**=emerging **D**=developing **I**=independent

Student: School Year:

PERSONAL NARRATIVE AND FICTION:	BEGINNING OF THE YEAR	MIDDLE OF THE YEAR	END OF THE YEAR
Identifies story elements.			
Describes the important events in a book.			
Understands how to retell a story using retelling language.			
Writes stories with a clear beginning, middle, and ending.			
Writes stories about personal experiences.			
Writes imaginative stories using story elements.			

NONFICTION:	BEGINNING OF THE YEAR	MIDDLE OF THE YEAR	END OF THE YEAR
Distinguishes fiction from nonfiction texts.			
Collects data, facts, and ideas from nonfiction texts (with support).			
Connects information from personal experiences to information in nonfiction texts (uses prior knowledge).			
Names and identifies specific nonfiction features (headings, labels, table of contents, photographs, captions, index, and glossary).			
Uses nonfiction features to navigate nonfiction text.			
Writes an all-about nonfiction book on a topic of interest.			

POETRY:	BEGINNING OF THE YEAR	MIDDLE OF THE YEAR	END OF THE YEAR
Distinguishes a poem from a story.			
Identifies common visual characteristics of poetry.			
Recognizes repetition in poetry.			
Attempts repetition in his or her own writing.			
Writes a poem based on the work of a mentor poet.			
Creates a simple visual image.			
Uses white space to convey the meaning of a poem.			

Complete 4 Component: Strategy First Grade

KEY: **E**=emerging **D**=developing **I**=independent

Student: School Year:

INPUT (the strategies readers use to comprehend text):	BEGINNING OF THE YEAR	MIDDLE OF THE YEAR	END OF THE YEAR
Uses prior knowledge, book cover, and the title to make thoughtful predictions about text.			
Understands how prediction can help us with comprehension of text.			
Identifies story elements.			
Retells using beginning, middle, and ending.			
Understands the term "character traits" and can name character traits in a book series.			
Compares characters across a series.			
Understands character's relation to a plot.			
Uses various strategies to read a new word.			
Monitors for meaning as he or she reads.			
Chooses level books to practice reading strategies.			
Models comprehension by talking about books with others.			

OUTPUT (the strategies writers use to create text):	BEGINNING OF THE YEAR	MIDDLE OF THE YEAR	END OF THE YEAR
Creates a story plan using plan sheets with pictures and words.			
Generates writing ideas.			
Adds to a story by adding details to pictures or writing more words.			
Shows knowledge of story elements by replicating them in his or her own writing.			
Can tell a story in order to prepare for writing a story.			
Uses his or her own experiences and passions to choose writing topics.			
Uses prior knowledge about a topic to add more to a story.			
Uses a set of spelling strategies to write unknown words.			
Uses mentor authors to write about characters.			

Complete 4 Component: Conventions First Grade

KEY: **E**=emerging **D**=developing **I**=independent

Student: _____   School Year: _____

SYNTAX:	BEGINNING OF THE YEAR	MIDDLE OF THE YEAR	END OF THE YEAR
Knowledge of when a sentence does not sound correct in reading.			
Knowledge of when a sentence does not sound correct in his or her own writing.			
Writes sentences using adjectives.			
Writes sentences with subject–verb agreement.			

PUNCTUATION:	BEGINNING OF THE YEAR	MIDDLE OF THE YEAR	END OF THE YEAR
Uses periods at end of sentences 85 percent of the time.			
Recognizes all other end-of-sentence punctuation in reading.			
Uses all other end-of-sentence punctuation.			
Recognizes internal punctuation (ellipses, quotation marks, commas).			
Uses capital letters at the beginning of sentences and for names.			
Uses primarily lowercase letters within a sentence.			
Leaves finger spaces between words.			

SPELLING/DECODING:	BEGINNING OF THE YEAR	MIDDLE OF THE YEAR	END OF THE YEAR
Accurately reads and spells known sight words.			
Incorporates known sight words into writing.			
Uses close approximation of hard words in reading and writing.			
Uses letter sounds to decode words.			
Uses word wall and other print in rooms to support spelling.			
Uses alphabet chart.			

Chapter 7

Essential Reading for the Complete 4 Educator

The Complete 4 for Literacy
by Pam Allyn

Pam's book *The Complete 4 for Literacy* introduces us to the idea of the four major components for literacy instruction: Process, Genre, Strategy, and Conventions. She illuminates the components and how they interact throughout the year. In your school communities, we encourage you to form study groups around these components. Begin with Pam's book and study it together to orient yourself. Then, each year or each season, select one of the components to focus on. We can use each component to discuss not just whole-class instruction but also how best to confer with individual students, how to work with struggling readers and writers, and how to assess our students. We have prepared a special selection of professional texts to foster your investigation of each of the components.

Writing Above Standard
by Debbie Lera

Debbie Lera will help you to frame a year of teaching writing that really helps your students soar using your state standards as a guide. With the Complete 4 as the backbone of her thinking, Debbie takes us on a journey through state standards and how to make them work for us. In the spirit of the Complete 4 and the Complete Year which is all about building flexible frameworks, this book furthers your thinking by helping you to benefit from the structure provided by the standards while attending to the individual needs of your students.

Professional Books on Process

There are wonderful classics in the field of the teaching of reading and writing that help remind us why process work is so critical. Learning routines, talking about books, choosing topics—these activities form the bedrock of a lifetime of success as readers and writers. Remind yourself that process is the key to a happy life: how you live your life is as important as what you do with it.

Some of our favorites include:

- *Becoming Literate: The Construction of Inner Control* by Marie M. Clay
- *First-Grade Writers: Units of Study to Help Children Plan, Organize, and Structure Their Ideas* by Stephanie Parsons
- *Growing Readers: Units of Study in the Primary Classroom* by Kathy Collins

Bonus:

- *Children's Books and Their Creators*, edited by Anita Silvey. A must-have for your shelf! This is a detailed collection of great authors' biographies and also excerpts from their most famous books. There is a lot of author information here that you can incorporate in the lessons about where writers get ideas.

Professional Books on Genre

First graders are capable of doing so much and are very proud of themselves for being like the big kids. Genre units allow our kindergarteners to try on many hats, and be in the world of reading and writing. Genre is a powerful tool. If you know which genre matches your purpose, you can communicate more effectively.

Helpful books for your learning include:

- *Climb Inside a Poem* by Georgia Heard and Lester Laminack
- *For the Good of the Earth and Sun* by Georgia Heard
- *Keepsakes: Using Family Stories in Elementary Classrooms* by Linda Winston
- *Nonfiction in Focus: A Comprehensive Framework for Helping Students Become Independent Readers and Writers of Nonfiction, K–6* by Janice V. Kristo and Rosemary A. Bamford

Professional Books on Strategy

In this book, you can see how strongly we believe in the strategic mind of the first grader! In his play, the first grader is thoughtful and bases his decisions on the whole of his idea. So, too, we can help our students become strategic as readers and writers. The following books contain some helpful information on strategy work:

- *Craft Lessons* by Ralph Fletcher
- *Fluency in Focus: Comprehension Strategies for All Young Readers* by Mary Lee Prescott-Griffin and Nancy I. Witherell
- *Guided Reading: Good First Teaching for All Children* by Irene C. Fountas and Gay Su Pinnell
- *Read It Again: Revisiting Shared Reading* by Brenda Parkes
- *Reading With Meaning: Teaching Comprehension in the Primary Grades* by Debbie Miller
- *Teaching for Comprehension in Reading, Grades K–2* by Gay Su Pinnell and Patricia L. Scharer
- *What Really Matters for Struggling Readers: Designing Research-Based Programs* by Richard Allington

Professional Books on Conventions

We are lucky that, in these last few years, there's been an explosion of interesting perspectives on the conventions of grammar, punctuation, and syntax. This is the hardest hurdle for us to overcome—most of us grew up remembering either no grammar instruction or terrible grammar instruction. Spelling and grammar and punctuation can all be fun, truly! Conventions instruction is empowering and students want to learn how to spell and they want to be in on the secrets of language.

Recommended books that focus on conventions include:

- *The Fluent Reader: Oral Reading Strategies for Building Word Recognition, Fluency, and Comprehension* by Timothy V. Rasinski
- *Mastering the Mechanics: Ready-to-Use Lessons for Modeled, Guided, and Independent Editing, K–1* by Linda Hoyt and Teresa Therriault
- *When Reading Begins: The Teacher's Role in Decoding, Comprehension, and Fluency* by Ardith Davis-Cole
- *Word Matters: Teaching Phonics and Spelling in the Reading and Writing Classroom* by Gay Su Pinnell and Irene C. Fountas
- *Words Their Way: Word Study for Phonics, Vocabulary, and Spelling Instruction* by Donald R. Bear, Marcia Invernizzi, Shane Templeton, and Francine Johnson

Resource Sheets

Early Fall
- Resource 2.1   The Four Prompts and Our Ideas
- Resource 2.2   Wondering Plan
- Resource 2.3   Remembering Plan
- Resource 2.4   Imagination Plan
- Resource 2.5   Observation Plan
- Resource 2.6   The Four Prompts Homework
- Resource 2.7   The Four Prompts Unit Assessment

Late Fall
- Resource 3.1   Our Own Character Traits
- Resource 3.2   Character Homework
- Resource 3.3   Physical Traits: What Your Character Looks Like
- Resource 3.4   Personality Trait Plan
- Resource 3.5   Character Reading Homework
- Resource 3.6   What Is Your Character Thinking?
- Resource 3.7   Character Comparison: Main and Secondary Characters
- Resource 3.8   Character Comparison: Main and You
- Resource 3.9   Character Web
- Resource 3.10 What We Have Learned
- Resource 3.11 Possible Titles
- Resource 3.12 Editing Checklist

Winter
- Resource 4.1   Nonfiction Features Chart One
- Resource 4.2   Nonfiction Features Chart Two
- Resource 4.3   Questions About Our Topic
- Resource 4.4   Picture Search

- Resource 4.5   Nonfiction Fact Sheet
- Resource 4.6   Nonfiction Homework
- Resource 4.7   Nonfiction Feature Detectives
- Resource 4.8   Feature Detectives Comparison
- Resource 4.9   Vocabulary Detectives
- Resource 4.10 Nonfiction Vocabulary Homework
- Resource 4.11 Nonfiction Project Plan
- Resource 4.12 Writing Topic
- Resource 4.13 Big Ideas Plan
- Resource 4.14 Big Idea/Heading 1
- Resource 4.15 Big Idea/Heading 2
- Resource 4.16 Big Idea/Heading 3
- Resource 4.17 Big Idea/Heading 4
- Resource 4.18 Nonfiction Research Questions Homework
- Resource 4.19 Nonfiction Picture Search Homework

Spring
- Resource 5.1   Reading With Expression and Fluency Homework
- Resource 5.2   Fluency Unit Assessment
- Resource 5.3   Fluency and Conventions Writing Homework
- Resource 5.4   Print Type Homework
- Resource 5.5   Peer Editing
- Resource 5.6   Using Fluency and Phrasing Unit Reflection
- Resource 5.7   Writing Celebration Comments

Name _____ Date _____

The Four Prompts and Our Ideas

Writers can use the Four Prompts to help them get ideas. Your writing work today is to look back at some older pieces of writing and think about where you may have gotten your ideas. Write the titles of your pieces in the appropriate boxes below.

I wonder	I remember

I imagine	I observe

Wondering Plan

Writers are always wondering about the world around them. This is one of the ways that a writer can get ideas. Write some of your wonderings in the wonder bubbles below.

Name _____ Date _____

Remembering Plan

Our memories can give us ideas for our writing.

Write a different memory in each one of the boxes below.

I remember when

I remember when

I remember when

I remember when

I remember when

I remember when

I remember when

Imagination Plan

Writers use their imagination to get ideas. In the clouds below, use your imagination to think about two new ideas.

Name _____ Date _____

Observation Plan

Writers observe the world very carefully. This helps a writer to get ideas. In the boxes below, use your senses to observe the world around you to help you get some new ideas for writing!

I see	I hear

I smell	I touch

I taste	I notice

Name _____ Date _____

The Four Prompts Homework

We have been learning that writers can get ideas by using the Four Prompts: I wonder, I remember, I imagine, and I observe. Tonight for homework, see if you can respond to each of the Four Prompts. Try to think of new ideas that you have not already written at school.

I wonder

I remember

I imagine

I observe

The Four Prompts Unit Assessment

(For use during a conference or at the end of the unit of study for your records.) Put a check mark under the prompt each child used and/or continues to use in his or her writing.

Name of Student	Wonder	Remember	Imagine	Observe

Name _____ Date _____

Our Own Character Traits

We all have something about our personality that makes us special. Today, think about yourself. What is one of your character traits? Write the special thing in the box below. Then write three things to prove you are that way.

I am:

Proof 1

Proof 2

Proof 3

Character Homework

We are beginning to study characters. We have spent time talking about ourselves and some of our personality traits, as well as some characters in books and their traits. Your reading work tonight is to think about one of your family members. Write down this family member's character trait and then prove it.

For example, I know that my mom is sensitive:

> 1. She cries a lot.
>
> 2. She loves to make other people feel good.
>
> 3. She understands when I feel sad and makes me feel better.

Name of Person _____

Personality Trait _____

Proof 1	**Proof 2**	**Proof 3**

Physical Traits: What Your Character Looks Like

Characters look different on the outside. Your study-group work today is to look closely at your character. Draw a picture of your character and label some of his/her physical traits.

Name of Character _____

Personality Trait Plan

A character has certain traits, just like we do. Your study-group work today is to find one trait about your character. Prove it!

Name of Character _____

Personality Trait _____

Proof 1	**Proof 2**	**Proof 3**

Name _____ Date _____

Character Reading Homework

We are beginning to study characters. We have spent time talking about ourselves and some of our personality traits, as well as some characters in books and their traits. Your reading work tonight is to think about one of the characters in the books you read. Write down one thing about the character's personality. Then prove it.

For example, as a class we have been reading books by Kevin Henkes. We decided that the character Lilly is creative. Our proof that she is creative:

   1. She makes fun costumes.

   2. She likes to pretend she is the queen.

   3. She makes funny faces with fruit on her sandwiches.

Name of Book _____

Name of Character _____

Personality Trait _____

Proof 1	**Proof 2**	**Proof 3**

What Is Your Character Thinking?

We have been studying a character. We are using what we already know about our characters to think about what they may do. Your work today is to try to figure out what your character is thinking.

Name of Character _____

Character Comparison:
Main and Secondary Characters

Main Character _____   Secondary Character _____

Name _____ Date _____

Character Comparison: Main and You

Main Character _____ You _____

Character Web

Your study-group work today is to create a web with as many character traits as you can think of to describe your character. Have fun!

Character's Name:

_____

Study Group Members _____

What We Have Learned

Over the past few weeks you and your character club have learned a lot about your character. In the boxes below, tell about some of the things you have learned.

Name of Character _____

Character Traits	**Character Actions**
How the Character Solves Problems	**Our Favorite Thing About This Character Is**

Possible title for a new book to add to the series:

_____

_____

RESOURCE 3.10

Study Group Members _____

Possible Titles

Name of Main Character _____

Name of Secondary Characters _____

Possible Titles for a New Book for the Character Series

1. _____

2. _____

3. _____

Title of Book	Kickoff	Event
Event	**Event**	**Tie-Up**

Study Group Members _____

Editing Checklist

Title of Book _____

- ❏ We have spaces between our words.

- ❏ We checked for mostly lowercase letters in our words.

- ❏ We used a capital I when the word is by itself.

- ❏ We have periods or question marks or exclamation points at the end of our sentences.

- ❏ We have uppercase letters at the beginning of our sentences.

- ❏ We have a cover.

- ❏ Our cover has a title.

- ❏ Our names are on the cover.

- ❏ Our pictures match our words.

Nonfiction Features Chart One

Name It	Where I Found It	What Does It Tell Me?
label		
heading		
photograph		
caption		
diagram		
maps		

Nonfiction Features Chart Two

Name It	Where I Found It	What Does It Tell Me?
index		
glossary		
table of contents		
fact box		
map key		
bold print		

Study Group Members _____

Questions About Our Topic

Our nonfiction study topic is _____

Please write two questions about your topic that you would like to find the answers to during our week-long study. Remember to think about your questions carefully and to work together as a group! We will find the answers as we learn more about our topic during the week.

Question 1: _____
_____

Answer:

Question 2: _____
_____

Answer:

Study Group Members _____

Picture Search

Our nonfiction study topic is _____

Nonfiction text gives us information. The pictures can give us a lot of information, too. Today your job is to:

      1. Pick ONE picture from one of your books.

      2. Study the picture.

      3. List four things you notice just from looking at the picture.

The picture is _____

Study Group Members _____

Nonfiction Fact Sheet

Study Group Topic _____

Your job today is to look in your nonfiction books for some new facts. A fact is something we know is true. Today, work with your group to find some new facts about your topic. Write the facts in the fact boxes below.

Fact Box 1

Fact Box 2

Fact Box 3

Fact Box 4

Name _____   Date _____

Nonfiction Homework

We have been learning all about nonfiction books and how to read them. We have found that nonfiction books have a lot of facts. Remember, a fact is something we can prove is true. Tonight for homework, look for two facts that you did not know before and write them below.

Title of Nonfiction Text _____

Fact (something that we know is true)	What does this make me think?

Fact (something that we know is true)	What does this make me think?

Name _____ Date _____

Nonfiction Feature Detectives

Title of Book _____

Feature:	I found it (smiley face here)	Page number
title page		
table of contents		
headings		
bold print		
captions		
photographs		
labels		
diagrams		
maps		
map key		
fact boxes		
close-ups		
index		
glossary		

Study Group Members _____

Feature Detectives Comparison

Study Group Topic _____

Your job today is to compare your feature detective work from yesterday with group members. Using yesterday's feature search, work with your group to see which features are the same in your books and which features are different.

If you have the feature put a 😊. If not, put an X.

	Book Title			
	Book 1	**Book 2**	**Book 3**	**Book 4**
Feature:				
title page				
table of contents				
headings				
bold print				
captions				
photographs				
labels				
diagrams				
maps				
map key				
fact boxes				
close-ups				
index				
glossary				

Vocabulary Detectives

Study Group Topic _____

Your job today is to be nonfiction vocabulary detectives!

Vocabulary words are words we use and understand. Sometimes when vocabulary in a book is new or hard we can:

- use words around the tricky word to help
- check the pictures
- ask what makes sense
- think about what we already know
- look in a dictionary

In the chart below, list four new words you found in ONE of your study-group topic books. Try to figure out the meaning by using the strategies above.

Vocabulary Word	Definition

Name _____ Date _____

Nonfiction Vocabulary Homework

We have been talking about learning new vocabulary. Remember, vocabulary words are words we use and understand. Sometimes when vocabulary in a book is new or hard we can:

- use words around the tricky word to help
- check the pictures
- ask what makes sense
- think about what we already know
- look in a dictionary

Tonight for homework, look through the nonfiction book you brought home. Make a list of four new vocabulary words you found in your book. Write them below. Then use the strategies above to help you figure out what the word means. You can also ask an adult to help you if you try and cannot figure out what the word means.

Vocabulary Word	Definition

Study Group Members _____

Nonfiction Project Plan

Study Group Topic _____

We have spent the past few weeks studying one topic. Today your group needs to think of a way to show what you have learned. Please discuss and decide how you want to show your learning on a poster. Please plan what you want to include below. Remember to use nonfiction features in your plan.

Name _____ Date _____

Writing Topic

Your writing work today is to think of four possible topics you may want to use for your nonfiction book. Remember to think of topics you know a lot about and feel strongly about. Circle the one you decide you are going to use as your topic after spending some time thinking about it.

Topic 1

Topic 2

Topic 3

Topic 4

Name _____

Date _____

Big Ideas Plan

Think about four big ideas you want as headings for your book.

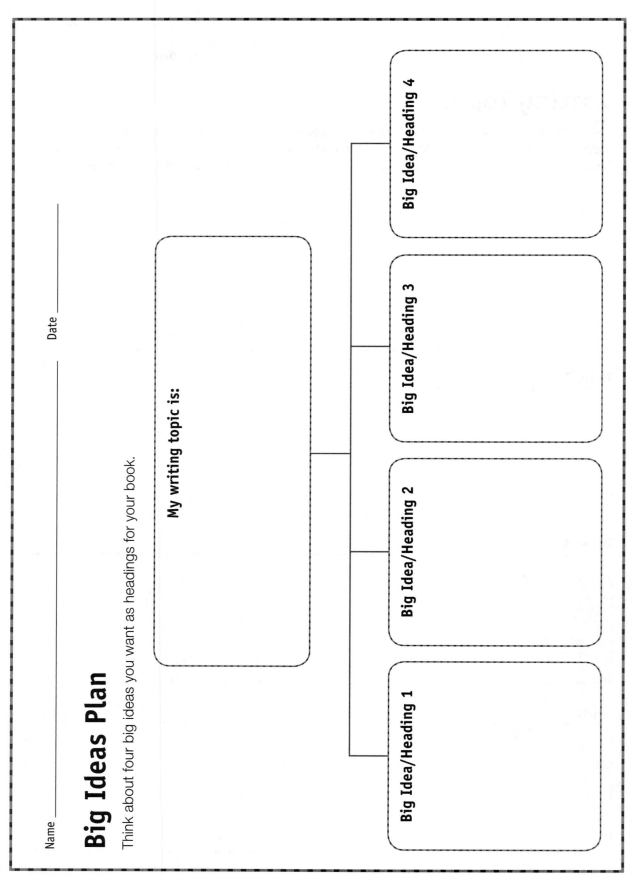

My writing topic is:

Big Idea/Heading 1

Big Idea/Heading 2

Big Idea/Heading 3

Big Idea/Heading 4

Name _____

Date _____

Big Idea/Heading 1

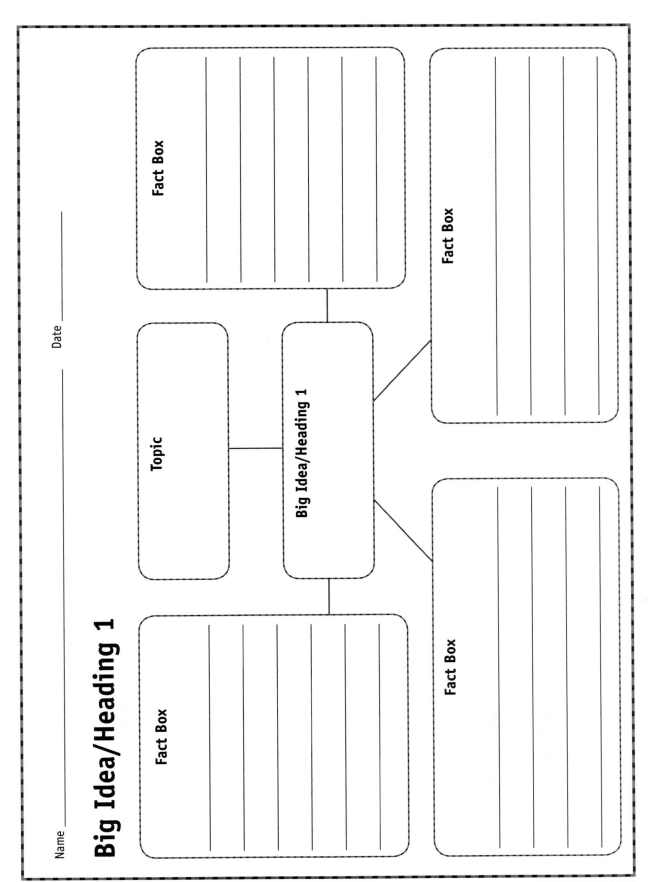

Topic

Big Idea/Heading 1

Fact Box

Fact Box

Fact Box

Fact Box

Big Idea/Heading 2

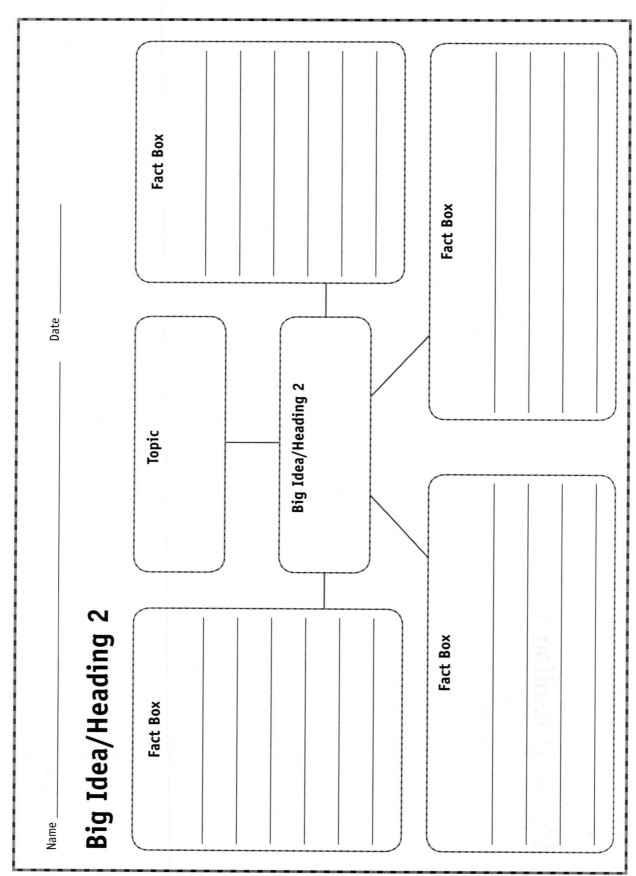

Topic

Big Idea/Heading 2

Fact Box

Fact Box

Fact Box

Fact Box

Name _____

Big Idea/Heading 3

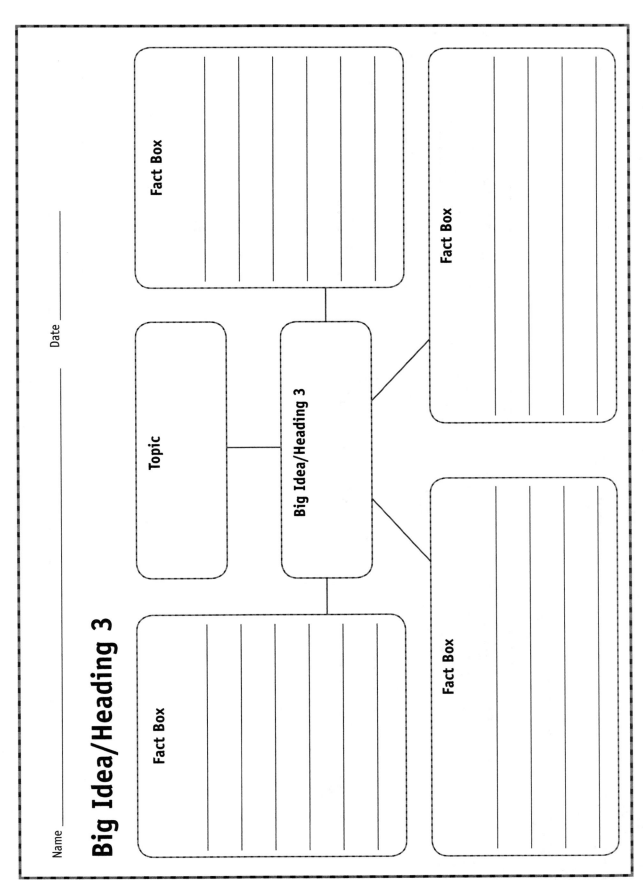

Topic

Big Idea/Heading 3

Fact Box

Fact Box

Fact Box

Fact Box

Big Idea/Heading 4

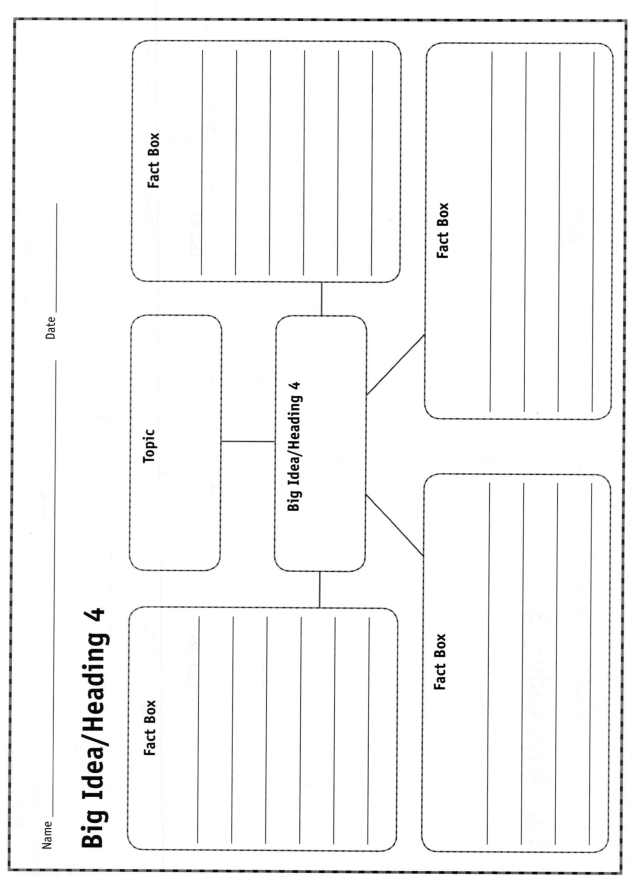

Topic

Big Idea/Heading 4

Fact Box

Fact Box

Fact Box

Fact Box

Nonfiction Research Questions Homework

We are working really hard on our nonfiction writing. We already know a lot about our topics, but we also know that we could find out more information by researching questions about our topics. Your job for homework is to research the questions we wrote in class. To find the answers you may use one or more of the resources below:

Interview

Interview someone whom you think would know the answer to one of your questions. For example, if you are writing about ballet, you may want to interview your ballet teacher. If you are writing about cooking you may want to interview your mom or dad. Choose someone who is an expert on your topic.

Internet

Look up your questions on the Internet. You can type a question into a search engine and you will see links to many of websites where you may find the answer.

Books and Magazines

Reference books about your topic could give you the answers you need to your questions. Other nonfiction books may also have the answers. Sometimes magazines may have the answers, too. Some good magazines for kids are *Time for Kids*, *National Geographic for Kids*, and *Your Big Backyard*. You can visit your local library to find other magazines.

TV/DVD

Sometimes you can find DVDs about your topic at the library. There are also specials on some of the learning channels on TV that might give you more information about your topic.

Have fun researching! Remember, your job is to answer the four questions you wrote in class.

Name _____ Date _____

Nonfiction Research Questions Homework

Nonfiction Topic _____

Question:	Question:
Answer:	Answer:
What research method did you use to get your answer?	**What research method did you use to get your answer?**
Question:	Question:
Answer:	Answer:
What research method did you use to get your answer?	**What research method did you use to get your answer?**

Nonfiction Picture Search Homework

Many nonfiction books have photographs. Your writing homework over the next few nights is to collect photographs that match your topic and your headings.

My writing topic is: _____

My four big ideas/headings are:

1. _____

2. _____

3. _____

4. _____

There are many places you can find photographs or pictures for your nonfiction books. You can look:

1. on the Internet

2. in old magazines (that your parents will let you cut up)

3. at photographs your family has taken (for example, if your topic is ballet, you may have a picture of yourself doing ballet)

Please bring as many photographs as you can to school, in a plastic bag. We will then use these pictures or photographs for our final copies of our books.

If you have trouble, we can look for some in school at the computer lab or in some of the classroom magazines.

Name _____   Date _____

Reading With Expression and Fluency Homework

We are learning how using punctuation helps us to read fluently and read like we talk. When we see the following punctuation marks, it changes our voice.

.	period	take a breath
,	comma	pause
!	exclamation point	show excitement, anger, surprise...
?	question mark	asks a question, voice goes up
...	ellipsis	more is coming...your voice goes longer
" "	quotation marks	someone is talking, change your voice
—	dash	a quick break in a sentence—pause
:	colon	used before you make a list

Your reading work tonight is to be punctuation detectives, and change how your voice sounds based on what you see. Show one of the places where your voice changed the most (write the words from the book) on the lines below. Make sure you also write the punctuation!

_____

_____

_____

_____

_____

_____

_____

_____

Name _____ Date _____

Fluency Unit Assessment

Check in the boxes below the punctuation or print type you think your partner is using as he or she reads. After he or she finishes reading, go over the reading piece and see if your guesses match the actual punctuation and/or print type.

Type of Punctuation (Listen to your partner as he or she reads. Think about how the reading sounds and what you know about how punctuation changes how we read.)			I think my partner had this in his or her reading piece. ☺	We checked the piece, and this is what was actually there. ✔
.	period	end of a sentence, breath		
,	comma	short pause		
?	question mark	asks a question, voice goes up		
!	exclamation point	show surprise, anger		
. . .	ellipsis	sounds like more is coming		
" "	quotation marks	someone is talking		

Print Type (Listen to your partner as he or she reads. Think about how the reading sounds and what you know about how print type changes how we read.)	I think my partner had this in his or her reading piece. ☺	We checked the piece, and this is what was actually there. ✔
bold		
CAPITALS		
italics		
colorful words		
small words		
BIG WORDS		
word bubbles		

Name _____ Date _____

Fluency and Conventions Writing Homework

We have been learning how punctuation changes our writing and makes it easier for the reader to understand. We can show emphasis using different types of punctuation. We can show that we are happy or sad, angry or surprised. We can show that more is coming.

Your writing work tonight is to look at my writing below. See if you can put in punctuation in the places I have missed. Remember, you can use periods, commas, question marks, exclamation points, and ellipses. Think about what you are reading and what would make sense and show the kind of emphasis you think I mean. Have an adult read it with you if the words are tricky.

The Ferry Ride

I was so excited It was my first time to ever ride a ferry that carried cars There were many different kinds of cars station wagons two doors four doors and many different colors blue yellow red green black and white I could not believe that all of these cars were going to fit on one boat What an amazing sight I would think that the boat would sink with all of this weight on it but it doesn't it FLOATS

As the cars loaded on my brother and I got very excited It was almost our turn to drive on My dad told us to be patient but it was really hard to hold back our excitement CLANG CLANG was the noise we heard as everyone drove on Finally it was our turn CLANG CLANG went the car as we bounced up onto the ramp and drove into the darkness of the bottom of the boat

Name _____ Date _____

Print Type Homework

We have been learning how print type can change the way we read. It can make our voice get louder or softer. It can use word bubbles to show that someone is talking with word bubbles. It can makes us read something with emphasis or without emphasis. Your writing homework is to draw a picture in the box below and then write some words to match your picture. Try to use many different print types in your picture and words from the chart below. Have fun!

Print type changes the way we read.	Draw your picture here.
BOLD CAPITALS *Italics* Colorful letters small and BIG words word bubbles	

Remember to use words to match your picture and try some different print types.

_____

_____

_____

_____

_____

_____

_____

Name _____ Date _____

Peer Editing

Name of Friend for Peer Editing _____

I noticed that my friend used the following punctuation and print type:

Punctuation		I found it! 😊	Print type	I found it! 😊
period	.		**bold** print	
comma	,		CAPITALS	
question mark	?		*italics*	
exclamation point	!		colorful letters	
ellipsis	. . .		small and BIG words	
quotation marks	" "		word bubbles	

Here is the punctuation and print type we added:

Punctuation		Added! 😊	Print type	Added! 😊
period	.		**bold** print	
comma	,		CAPITALS	
question mark	?		*italics*	
exclamation point	!		colorful letters	
ellipsis	. . .		small and BIG words	
quotation marks	" "		word bubbles	

Rate your peer editing. How did you and your friend work together?

GREAT   **Pretty Good**   **Okay**

Name _____ Date _____

Using Fluency and Phrasing Unit Reflection

We have spent the past two weeks making our writing better by adding punctuation and print type. Take a few minutes to look at the writing that you worked on.

What is your favorite sentence where you used new punctuation? Write it below.

_____

_____

_____

_____

_____

_____

What is your favorite sentence where you used a new print type? Write it below.

_____

_____

_____

_____

_____

_____

Writing Celebration Comments

Cut along the lines.

Your Name: **Reader's Name:** **Comment:**	**Your Name:** **Reader's Name:** **Comment:**
Your Name: **Reader's Name:** **Comment:**	**Your Name:** **Reader's Name:** **Comment:**

Glossary of Terms for the Complete Year Series

We try to avoid jargon as much as possible, but it is inevitable that a community creates or uses specific terminology to identify important aspects of its work. We want you to feel comfortable with all the language inside this book. What follows are some of the key words we have used throughout this book and throughout the Complete Year series.

Anchor texts These are the books that moor us to the places of our learning. An anchor holds a ship in place, in water that may be moving fast. Texts are like that for us in our teaching. We are in moving water all the time, but great literature anchors us down to our teaching, to our learning, to our goals and outcomes. Anchor texts connect us to the teaching inside our units of study. They keep our teaching on course, steady, focused, anchoring our big ideas, our commitments and indeed, the essence of each unit. Anchor texts may also be used throughout the year in both the teaching of reading and the teaching of writing. For example, one text may be used in a reading unit for retelling, or sensory image, or prediction. The same text may also be used as a demonstration text for writing with detail, strong leads and endings, and the use of dialogue. There are some special texts that can travel with you throughout the year. They are great, lasting titles that transcend any one teaching point. These are considered anchor texts for the year.

Book clubs Working in book clubs allows students to build their collaboration skills and their ability to talk about texts. Book clubs may form from two sets of successful partnerships, or for a variety of teaching purposes. You may group a club according to skill sets or according to interests. Students in a club do not all have to be reading the same book. For example, in a nonfiction unit, the students may meet to discuss editorials or historical writing, using different texts at their own reading levels. You should give clear guidelines for the purposes of a club, its duration, expected outcomes, and how it will be assessed.

Commitment The fourth stage of a unit of study, the Commitment stage, is the bridge from the end of one unit to the beginning of the next one. Look for and make public examples of student work and behaviors that are becoming more integrated into the ongoing work of the individual and the community.

This stage asks the question: How is what we have learned in this unit going to inform our learning as we begin the next one? It also requires a response to the question: What have you learned?

Conferences/conferring This is a process for informally assessing your students' progress, and for differentiating your instruction for individual readers and writers. Ideally, you will meet with each student at least once a week in a brief, focused conference session. Stages of a conference are:

- **Preread/Research** (be very familiar with your student's work and processes in advance of the conference)
- **Ask** (pertinent questions relating to your lesson, the ongoing work, and the plans going forward)
- **Listen** (take notes, with attention to next steps)
- **Teach** (one target point)
- **Plan** (what the student will do when you leave the conference: today, tomorrow, throughout the unit and the year)

Conventions The fourth component of the Complete 4, Conventions refers to grammar, punctuation, and syntax. Understanding the conventions of the English language has a direct impact on reading comprehension and writing mechanics and fluency.

Downhill texts These are texts we can rest and relax into—to practice building our stamina or our fluency or to revisit favorite characters, authors, or series. They are books that do not require a great deal of decoding to be done by the reader, as the text is generally below the reader's independent reading level.

Focused Instruction The first part of every day's reading and writing time, Focused Instruction is the short, focused lesson at the beginning of each workshop session in the teaching of reading or writing. Each lesson should build on the ones before it. No lesson is taught in isolation.

Four Prompts In order to help our students learn how to find ideas for writing, we have developed a set of prompts to guide them. They are I wonder, I remember, I observe, and I imagine. You can use these to support your students' writing in any genre.

Genre The second component of the Complete 4, Genre typically refers to a type of text such as poetry, nonfiction, or narrative. Within each of these genres are subgenres, which may include a specific focus on persuasive nonfiction writing, or informational nonfiction writing in nonfiction studies. In a narrative study, the focus might be on the short story, the memoir, or story elements. We want students to focus on how they engage with a particular genre. How do we read a newspaper, for example, and how do we read a poem? How are they different, and how are they the same? We will talk about uses for a genre, the reasons we read inside one genre for a length of time, and how our thinking grows and changes as a result of that immersion.

Guided Practice In the third stage of any unit of study, Guided Practice, we use mentor texts, transcripts, teacher or student writing, think-alouds, role plays, and read-alouds to model exemplary attributes, behaviors, and qualities related to the unit. Over the course of this stage, students are given increasing responsibility for this work. It is generally the longest stage of a unit, as all students need time for practice.

Identification The second stage of any unit of study, Identification, is the time when we begin to develop the common language we will use throughout the study. We identify attributes of a genre, behaviors in a process, qualities of a craft element, rules for a convention or mark. Our thinking is recorded in public charts, student writing notebooks, and our notebook.

Immersion The first stage of any unit of study, Immersion, is the initial period of inquiry during which we surround our students with the sounds, textures, and qualities of a Genre, Process, Strategy, or Conventions focus. We marinate our students in the literature, the actions and reflections, and the attention to detail and conventions that are part of the study. During this stage, students construct a working understanding of the topic under discussion.

Independent Practice Following each day's Focused Instruction, Independent Practice provides time for students to read or write independently and authentically. Students independently read a variety of texts matched to their reading levels. Students also write a variety of texts independently, depending on the unit and their ability levels. They practice the skills and strategies taught in the whole-group sessions. We provide daily lessons to support their work, and confer regularly with the students to assess their individual needs.

Mentor text Somewhat interchangeable with an anchor text, we are more inclined to use mentor text to describe books that have particular appeal to individual students. Mentor texts inspire students' reading and writing, whereas anchor texts are specific texts chosen in advance by the teacher to prepare a unit. So in a poetry unit, one mentor text might be a Langston Hughes poem, "The Dream Keeper," because the student loves it and wants to write like that, whereas another student might choose a Valerie Worth poem because she likes the brevity of her language.

Partnerships At times you may choose to pair children for different reasons and different lengths of time. Partnerships can be very fluid, lasting for just one session, a week, or an entire unit. Partnerships may be based on reading levels, similar interests in particular books or subjects, or because you would like to work with the partners on a regular basis on small instructional reading or writing work.

Process The first of the Complete 4 components, Process asks readers and writers to become aware of their habits and behaviors, and to move forward in developing them. Process units can investigate roles, routines, capacity, or collaboration.

Read-aloud During read-aloud, you read from carefully chosen texts that reflect the reading and writing work the community is doing together. Listening to fluent and expressive read-alouds helps students identify the many aspects of text and develop their own deeper understandings of Process, Genre, Strategy, or Conventions. You may read from a book or short text that illustrates the topic of the Focused Instruction for the day, and encourage students to pursue that thinking in their independent reading and writing. During and at the end of the read-aloud, the whole class may have a conversation relating to the ideas in the story.

Reading notebook *See* Writing Notebook.

Shared reading/shared writing During this activity, you and your students read together from a shared text (on an overhead, chart, or a SMART Board, or using copies of the text). While teachers of younger children use shared reading and writing to help build decoding skills, teachers of older children may use shared reading to teach word analysis, new vocabulary, or punctuation skills. It's also a good way to work with older students on big-picture thinking such as developing an idea about a text, asking questions, or making inferences. Teachers of older students may use shared writing to guide their students toward new writing strategies in a public writing context, or model use of details and elaboration to improve their writing.

Small instructional groups This structure is used to differentiate and direct instruction to the specific needs of a small group of learners. You pull small groups of readers or writers with similar needs to explicitly teach targeted reading and writing skills. You select and introduce the texts for reading and make specific teaching points. You may prompt students in small writing groups to do a short, focused writing exercise based on their needs. These groups are flexible and will change as the year unfolds.

Stages of the lesson Each day, we should work with our students in a whole-small-whole routine. First we bring everyone together for the lesson (see Focused Instruction), then we send students off to practice something we have taught (see Independent Practice), and finally we call them back to join us for a recap and reiteration of our teaching (see Wrap-Up).

Stages of the unit Each unit of study follows a progression of instruction, from Immersion to Identification to Guided Practice to Commitment. These stages provide students with the necessary opportunities to notice, name, practice, and share their learning—all of which contribute to a deeper understanding and application of our teaching (see Immersion, Identification, Guided Practice, and Commitment).

Steady reader or writer This student is making steady progress and meeting appropriate grade-level expectations.

Strategy The third component in the Complete 4, Strategy consists of two types: reading and writing. In reading, Strategy refers to individual or grouped strategies for reading comprehension that impact reading development. These include visualizing, synthesizing, questioning, and inferring. A unit focused on strategy can be embedded in another study or illuminated on its own. Strategy units also include the study of theme, interpretation, building an argument, and story elements. In writing, Strategy refers to craft. This may include the external or internal structures of writing. Units in writing strategy may include structures of nonfiction or narrative texts, a focus on a particular author, or, internally, units focused on the use of repetition, varied sentence length, or the artful use of punctuation.

Strong reader or writer This student is performing above grade-level expectations.

Turn and talk This common technique helps students warm up for their reading or writing work. By asking students to "turn and talk" to someone in the meeting area to rehearse their thoughts, we give all students a chance to have their voices heard. It is an effective management technique for making sure students are prepared for the work ahead.

Unit of study A one- to six-week period of intensive study on one aspect of reading or writing. The Complete 4 curriculum planning system helps teachers and administrators plan an entire school year in the teaching of reading and writing.

Uphill texts This descriptor refers to a text that is above a student's independent reading level. Sometimes we want our readers to challenge themselves with a harder text. Sometimes readers have very good reasons for why they would like to keep an uphill book close by. Other times, though, we ask them to recognize that the book is too uphill for the task, and that they need to find a level text with which they can feel successful.

Vulnerable reader or writer This describes the reader or writer who struggles to keep up with the demands of the grade level. These are students who need extra support and scaffolding through appropriate texts or individualized or small-group instruction. Our vulnerable readers and writers need special care to feel successful and to flourish in our classrooms.

Wrap-Up The final step in each day's reading or writing time, the Wrap-Up is when we ask our students to return to a whole-group setting for reflection and reinforcement. For example, you may share one or two examples of student work or student behaviors ("Today I noticed . . . "), or one or two students might briefly share their thinking processes or the work itself.

Writing clubs These are recommended for all ages. Children may create clubs based on common interests, from the block area and writing in kindergarten to mystery writing in fourth grade. Give clear guidelines for the purposes of the clubs, the length of time they will last, the expectations, the outcomes, and how you will assess the progress of each club.

Writing notebook/reading notebook/ writing folder/reading folder These are containers for thinking and tools for collecting ideas, wonderings, observations, questions, research, lists, snippets of texts, and responses to literature. The form of the container is not the important thing; what is important is having containers for student work that make sense to your students and work well for you in terms of collecting and preserving a history of student reading and writing.

Grade 1 Anchor Texts

Early Fall

The ARCH: Building Independence: Reading Role Models

- *All Pigs Are Beautiful* by Dick King-Smith
- *The Best Place to Read* by Debbie Bertram
- *A Book About Bears* by Mel Berger
- *Bread and Jam for Frances* by Russell Hoban
- *The Carrot Seed* by Ruth Krauss
- *Do Like Kyla* by Angela Johnson
- *In the Land of Words* by Eloise Greenfield
- *Inch by Inch* by Leo Lionni
- *Little Bear* by Else Minarik
- *Reading Makes You Feel Good* by Todd Parr
- *The Recess Queen* by Alexis O'Neill
- *Sophie and Sammy's Library Sleepover* by Judith Caseley
- *The Teeny Tiny Teacher* by Stephanie Calmenson
- "Under the Sunday Tree" in *Under the Sunday Tree* by Eloise Greenfield
- *Wild About Books* by Judy Sierra

The ARCH: Building Independence: Writing Role Models

- *Dear Annie* by Judith Caseley
- *Hair Dance!* by Dinah Johnson
- *My Map Book* by Sara Fanelli
- *The Racecar Alphabet* by Brian Floca
- *The Seashore Book* by Charlotte Zolotow
- *Under the Sunday Tree* by Eloise Greenfield
- *Voices of the Heart* by Ed Young

Developing Print Strategies

- Emergent Big Books or poems that can be used to show how to solve new words such as *Mrs. Wishy-Washy's Tub* by Joy Cowley and *Who's in the Tub?* by Sylvia M. Jones
- *Snow Day!* by Lester Laminack

Conveying Messages: Signs and Letters

Anchor texts that show how there are different kinds of writing in the world including:

- *A Book of Letters* by Ken Wilson-Max
- *Clarice Bean, That's Me* by Lauren Child
- *Click, Clack, Moo: Cows That Type* by Doreen Cronin
- *Dear Mrs. LaRue* by Mark Teague
- *I Read Signs* by Tana Hoban
- *With Love, Little Red Hen* by Alma Flor Ada

Making Wise Book Choices

A classroom library filled with books in baskets that are easy for children to access; leveled books; books labeled by genre, author, and other categories; model texts at different levels for first graders such as:

- *Biscuit* by Alyssa Capucilli
- *Henry and Mudge* by Cynthia Rylant
- *Jambo Means Hello: Swahili Alphabet Book* by Muriel Feelings

Making Choices as Writers: The Four Prompts

- *Growing Frogs* by Vivian French and other Read and Wonder Series Books
- *Mei-Mei Loves the Morning* by Margaret Holloway Tsubakiyama
- *Night in the Country* by Cynthia Rylant
- *Snowmen at Night* by Carolyn Buehner
- *What If?* by Jonathan Shipton
- *Wilfred Gordon McDonald Partridge* by Mem Fox

Becoming Strong Partners: Reading Together

- *"Let's Get a Pup!" said Kate* by Bob Graham
- *Share and Take Turns* by Cheri J. Meiners and Meredith Johnson
- *Surprising Sharks* by Nicola Davis

Understanding Rules Writers Use

- *Along Comes Jake* or *Move Over* by Joy Cowley
- *Oh, Brother!* by Nikki Grimes and Mike Benny
- *Smash! Crash!* by Jon Scieszka
- *Who's in the Shed?* by Brenda Parkes

Late Fall

Growing a Sense of Story: Reading Fiction

- *Caps for Sale* by Esphyr Flobadkina
- *Elizabeti's Doll* by Stephanie Stuve-Bodeen
- *Froggy's Sleepover* and other Froggy books by Jonathan London
- *The Hatseller and the Monkeys* by Baba Wague Diakite
- *Lilly's the Purple Plastic Purse* by Kevin Henkes
- *Owen* by Kevin Henkes

Growing a Sense of Story: Writing Fiction

- *Elizabeti's Doll* by Stephanie Stuve-Bodeen
- *Froggy's Sleepover* and other Froggy books by Jonathan London
- *The Hatseller and the Monkeys* by Baba Wague Diakite
- *Lilly's Purple Plastic Purse* by Kevin Henkes
- *Owen* by Kevin Henkes

Making Meaning: Using Prediction to Further Our Thinking

- *Anansi the Spider: A Tale from the Ashanti* by Gerald McDermott
- *Giraffes Can't Dance* by Giles Anderea
- *Hannah Duck* by Angie Yamamura
- *"Let's Get a Pup!" said Kate* by Bob Graham
- *Muncha! Muncha! Muncha!* by Candace Fleming
- *Tacky the Penguin* and other Tacky books by Helen Lester

Building Stamina: Writing Long and Strong

- *Author: A True Story* by Helen Lester
- *How a Book Is Made* by Aliki
- *Nothing Ever Happens on 90th Street* by Roni Schotter
- *What Do Authors Do?* by Eileen Christelow

Becoming Strong Partners: Deepening Conversation

- *For You Are a Kenyan Child* by Kelly Cunnane
- *Kitten's First Full Moon* by Kevin Henkes
- *The Recess Queen* by Alexis O'Neill
- *Robots* by Clive Gifford

Investigating Character Traits in Series Books: Character Clubs

- Dragon books by Dav Pilkey
- Fluffy books by Kate McMullan
- Henry and Mudge books by Cynthia Rylant
- Olivia books by Ian Falconer
- Poppleton books by Cynthia Rylant
- *We Are All Alike, We Are All Different* by Todd Parr

Writing a New Series Book: Character Clubs

- Dragon books by Dav Pilkey
- Fluffy books by Kate McMullan
- Henry and Mudge books by Cynthia Rylant
- Olivia books by Ian Falconer
- Poppleton books by Cynthia Rylant

Winter

Navigating Nonfiction

- *A Field Full of Horses* by Peter Hansard
- *Meet the Octopus* by Sylvia James
- *Polar Lands* by Margaret Hynes
- *The Supermarket* by Kathleen Krull
- *Surprising Sharks* by Nicola Davies
- *What Do You Do With a Tail Like This?* by Robin Page and Steve Jenkins

Creating All-About Books: Nonfiction

- *Chameleons Are Cool* by Martin Jenkins
- *I Love Guinea Pigs* by Dick King-Smith
- *My Visit to the Aquarium* by Aliki
- *The Supermarket* by Kathleen Krull
- *Surprising Sharks* by Nicola Davies

Developing Print Strategies: Readers Reread and Revise

- *Amazing Grace* by Mary Hoffman
- *Bigmama's* by Donald Crews
- *A Weekend With Wendell* by Kevin Henkes
- *Yoko* by Rosemary Wells

Enhancing Our Writing: Revision Strategies

- *Some Things Change* by Mary Murphy

Making Meaning: Connecting Across Genres

- *A Book About Bears* by Mel Berger
- *Brown Bear, Brown Bear, What Do You See?* by Eric Carle and Bill Martin, Jr.
- *Fish Eyes* by Mia Ocean
- *Hello Fish!* by Sylvia Earle
- *I Read Signs* by Tana Hoban
- *The Rainbow Fish* by Marcus Pfister
- *Swimmy* by Leo Lionni
- *What's It Like to Be a Fish?* by Wendy Pfeffer

Spring

Sounding Like Readers: Fluency and Phrasing

- *Bark George* by Jules Feiffer
- *Has Anyone Seen William?* by Bob Graham
- *The Hungry Giant* by Joy Cowley
- *I Lost My Bear* by Jules Feiffer
- *Knuffle Bunny* by Mo Willems
- *Muncha! Muncha! Muncha!* by Candace Fleming
- *Wolf!* by Becky Bloom

Using Fluency and Phrasing to Enhance Our Writing

- *Bark George* by Jules Feiffer
- *Don't Let Pigeon Drive the Bus!* by Mo Willems
- *Move Over!* by Joy Cowley
- *The Night I Followed the Dog* by Nina Laden
- *Yo! Yes?* by Chris Raschka

Building Stamina: Reading Long and Strong

- *Animal Homes* by Bobbi Kalman
- *Biscuit* by Alyssa Capucilli
- "Dreams" by Langston Hughes (*The Collected Poems of Langston Hughes*)
- *Henry and Mudge and the Wild Wind* by Cynthia Rylant
- *The Legend of Mexicatl* by Jo Harper
- *Reading Makes You Feel Good* by Todd Parr

Becoming Strong Partners: Supporting Each Other as Writers

- *Big Al* by Andrew Clements and Yoshi

Exploring the Sound of Poetry

- "April Rain Song" and "Poem" by Langston Hughes (*The Collected Poems of Langston Hughes*)
- "Chairs" by Valerie Worth (*All the Small Poems and Fourteen More* by Valerie Worth)
- "Moon, Have You Seen My Mother?" by Karla Kuskin
- *Off the Sweet Shores of Africa and Other Talking Drum Rhymes* by Uzo Unobagha
- "Sick" by Shel Silverstein (*Where the Sidewalk Ends*)
- "Sliding Board" by Kay Winters (*Did You See What I Saw? Poems About School*)

Becoming Poets: Words That Sing

- "Her Daddy's Hands" by Angela Johnson (*In Daddy's Arms I Am Tall*)
- "One Inch Tall," by Shel Silverstein (*Where the Sidewalk Ends*)
- "Ready for Sleep" and "If You're Tired and You Know It" by Bruce Lansky (*Sweet Dreams: Bedtime Poems, Songs, and Lullabies*)
- "What I'd Cook for My Teacher," by Bruce Lansky (*If Pigs Could Fly*)

Looking Back, Looking Forward: Making Summer Reading Plans

- *Abuela* by Arthur Dorros
- *The Friendly Four* by Eloise Greenfield
- *What You Know First* by Patricia MacLachlan

Looking Back, Looking Forward: Making Summer Writing Plans

- *The Friendly Four* by Eloise Greenfield
- *The Night Before Summer Vacation* by Natasha Wing and Julie Durrell
- *The Pattaconk Brook* by James Stevenson

Professional References

Allington, R. (2005). *What really matters for struggling readers: Designing research-based programs.* Boston: Allyn & Bacon.

Allyn, P. (2007). *The complete 4 for literacy.* New York: Scholastic.

Anderson, C. (2000). *How's it going? A practical guide to conferring with student writers.* Portsmouth, NH: Heinemann.

Avery, C. (2002). *...And with a light touch: Learning about reading, writing, and teaching with first graders* (2nd ed.). Portsmouth, NH: Heinemann.

Bear, D., Invernizzi, M., Templeton, S., & Johnston, F. (2004). *Words their way: Word study for phonics, vocabulary and spelling Instruction.* Boston: Pearson Education.

Beaver, J. (2006). *DRA2: Developmental reading assignment.* Parsippany, NJ: Pearson Education.

Calkins, L. (1994). *The art of teaching writing.* Portsmouth, NH: Heinemann.

Clay, M. M. (1991). *Becoming literate: The construction of inner control.* Portsmouth, NH: Heinemann.

Clay, M. M. (1993). *Reading recovery: A guidebook for teachers in training.* Portsmouth, NH: Heinemann.

Clay, M. M. (2005). An *observation survey of early literacy achievement.* Portsmouth, NH: Heinemann.

Collins, K. (2004). *Growing readers: Units of study in the primary classroom.* Portland, ME: Stenhouse.

Davis-Cole, A. (2004). *When reading begins: The teacher's role in decoding, comprehension and fluency.* Portsmouth, NH: Heinemann.

Dragan, P. B. (2003). *Everything you need to know to teach first grade.* Portsmouth, NH: Heinemann.

Fletcher, R. (1992). *What a writer needs.* Portsmouth, NH: Heinemann.

Fletcher, R., & Portalupi, J. (2007). *Craft lessons: Teaching writing K–8.* Portland, ME: Stenhouse.

Fountas, I. C., & Pinnell G. S. (1996). *Guided reading: Good first teaching for all children.* Portsmouth, NH: Heinemann.

Fountas, I. C., & Pinnell G. S. (1998). *Word matters: Teaching phonics and spelling in the reading and writing classroom.* Portsmouth, NH: Heinemann.

Fountas, I. C., & Pinnell G. S. (1999). *Matching books to readers: Using leveled books in guided reading, K–3.* Portsmouth, NH: Heinemann.

Fountas, I. C., & Pinnell G. S. (2000). *Interactive writing: How language and literacy come together.* Portsmouth, NH: Heinemann.

Gentry, J. R. (2008). *Step-by-step assessment guide to code breaking.* New York: Scholastic.

Graves, D. (1994). *A fresh look at writing.* Portsmouth, NH: Heinemann.

Harvey, S., & Goudvis, A. (2000). *Strategies that work: Teaching comprehension for understanding and engagement.* Portland, ME: Stenhouse.

Heard, G. (1989). *For the good of the earth and sun: Teaching poetry.* Portsmouth, NH: Heinemann.

Hindley, J. (1996). *In the company of children.* Portland, ME: Stenhouse.

Hoyt, L. (2002). *Make it real: Strategies for success with informational text.* Portsmouth, NH: Heinemann.

Hoyt, L., & Therriault, T. (2008). *Mastering the mechanics, grades K–1: Ready-to-use lessons for modeled, guided, and independent editing.* New York: Scholastic.

Kristo, J. V., & Bamford, R. A. (2004). *Nonfiction in focus: A comprehensive framework for helping students become independent readers and writers of nonfiction, K–6.* New York: Scholastic.

Lera, D. (2009). *Writing above standard: Engaging lessons that take standards to new heights and help kids become skilled, inspired writers.* New York: Scholastic.

Miller, D. (2002). *Reading with meaning: Teaching comprehension in the primary grades.* Portland, ME: Stenhouse.

Moore, P., & Lyon, A. (2005). *New essentials for teaching reading in PreK–2.* New York: Scholastic.

Murray, D. (1982). *Learning by teaching.* Portsmouth, NH: Boynton/Cook.

Parkes, B. (2000). *Read it again! Revisiting shared reading.* Portland, ME: Stenhouse.

Parsons, S. (2005). *First-grade writers: Units of study to help children plan, organize, and structure their ideas.* Portsmouth, NH: Heinemann.

Pearson, D., & Gallagher, M. (1983). The instruction of reading comprehension. *Contemporary Educational Psychology, 8*(3),317–345.

Pinnell, G. S., & Scharer, P. L. (2003). *Teaching for comprehension in reading, grades K–2.* New York: Scholastic.

Prescott-Griffin, M. L., & Witherell, N. I. (2004). *Fluency in focus: Comprehension strategies for all young readers.* Portsmouth, NH: Heinemann.

Rasinski, T. V. (2003). *The fluent reader: Oral reading strategies for building word recognition, fluency, and comprehension.* New York: Scholastic.

Ray, K. W. (2004). *About the authors: Writing workshop for our youngest writers.* Portsmouth, NH: Heinemann.

Ray, K. W. (1999). *Wondrous words, writers and writing in the elementary classroom.* Urbana, IL: National Council of Teachers of English.

Rich, M. (2007, November 19). Study links drop in test scores to a decline in time spent reading. *New York Times*, pp. E1, E7.

Robb, L. (2003). *Literacy links: Practical strategies to develop the emergent literacy at-risk children need.* Portsmouth, NH: Heinemann.

Roser, N., & Martinez, M. (2005). *What a character! Character study as a guide to literacy meaning making in grades K–5.* Newark, DE: International Reading Association.

Silvey, A. (Ed.) (1995). *Children's books and their creators.* Boston: Houghton Mifflin.

Strunk, W., & White, E. B. (1999). *The elements of style* (4th ed.). New York: Longman.

Taberski, S. (2000). *On solid ground: Strategies for teaching reading K–3.* Portsmouth, NH: Heinemann.

Wilde, S. (2007). *Spelling strategies and patterns: What kids need to know.* Portsmouth, NH: Heinemann.